Praise for Thomas M. Sterne

"Thomas Sterner's work on practice has changed my life. ... Life Coach Instructor I have read many materials on self-help, mind management, habit development, and growth. I rate Tom's work to be among the very best of the hundreds of books I have studied. He teaches his brilliant concepts in a style that is easy to understand and implement. It doesn't matter what you want to get better at doing or being; Tom has the teachings that, when applied, will get you there. Study his work, learn and practice what he demonstrates, and you'll know more peace, productivity, and profit, guaranteed."

— **Brooke Castillo**, Master Certified Coach
and president of The Life Coach School

"Last year as a Techpreneur, living in the most disruptive and innovative period in history, I set for myself and completed a five-hundred-book personal growth challenge. I believe this challenge qualifies me to pay tribute to this extraordinary author, Thomas Sterner. Throughout this challenge, encountering a book able to significantly influence my life in as profound a manner as Tom's first book, *The Practicing Mind*, was exceptionally rare. It was clear that the wisdom shared in this work stemmed from solid reflection and a set of deeply entrenched values embedded in this master. Tom's work and ideas are beyond reproach, but what truly impressed me were his humility, authenticity, and generous spirit."

— **Alysia Silberg**, UN Women Empower Women Global
Champion for Women's Economic Empowerment.

Praise for Thomas Sterner's *The Practicing Mind*

"Thomas Sterner's brilliance shines through in the brevity of this complex book's pages.... This tiny but intense book delivers enough information to contemplate and apply for a lifetime."

— *Roundtable Reviews*

"Thomas Sterner, prompted by his experiences learning to play golf as an adult and as an accomplished musician, shares insights, stories, and advice for mastering the skills of our choosing with less frustration and more pleasure.... [*The Practicing Mind*] helps us understand exactly what present moment awareness is, how the culture we live in constantly instructs us to the contrary, and how we can change our mindset to make this a part of our daily life."

— *New Thought*

"Sterner's encouragement...is to find things that help us do well and practice them — staying in the moment, creating and practicing good habits, and being patient, disciplined, and even-tempered in our work."

— *The Horn Call*

"Thomas Sterner gives us a useful, thoughtful, much-needed book on the often-overlooked science and art of practice....Anyone hoping to excel at anything should read this."

— **Roy F. Baumeister**, coauthor of
Willpower: Rediscovering the Greatest Human Strength

"*The Practicing Mind* engagingly transforms difficulty into devotion, offering a practical, easy-to-understand approach that will transform your view of even the most challenging or mundane steps on your journey of life."

— **Marney K. Makridakis**, author of *Creating Time*
and founder of ArtellaLand.com

"Thomas Sterner's book has provided helpful information in all areas of my life. As a business leader, I became more effective; as a public speaker, more dynamic; as a parent, more attentive; and with my weekend hobbies, I learned to have more fun and increase skills."

— **Ralph Citino**, banking professional

"In *The Practicing Mind*, Tom Sterner achieves a rare combination: he provides not just a clear set of practical steps for creating focused effort but also a theoretical background that can help us to reframe our expectations and values so that we can keep in perspective the difference between process and product, progress and goals. Highly recommended."

— **Dr. Scott A. Davison**, professor of philosophy at Morehead State
University and author of *On the Intrinsic Value of Everything*

FULLY
ENGAGED

Also by Thomas M. Sterner

The Practicing Mind

FULLY ENGAGED

Using the Practicing Mind
in Daily Life

THOMAS M. STERNER

New World Library
Novato, California

New World Library
14 Pamaron Way
Novato, CA 94949

Text design by Tona Pearce Myers

Library of Congress Cataloging-in-Publication Data is available.

First printing, October 2016
ISBN 978-1-60868-432-8
Ebook ISBN 978-1-60868-433-5
Printed in Canada on 100% postconsumer-waste recycled paper

New World Library is proud to be a Gold Certified Environmentally Responsible Publisher. Publisher certification awarded by Green Press Initiative. www.greenpressinitiative.org

10   9   8   7   6   5   4   3   2   1

*This book is dedicated to my father,
Thomas D. Sterner. All those who have
enjoyed my work owe him a debt
of gratitude, for he taught me that it is never
"Can it be done?" but always "Just do it,
and you will figure it out along the way."
His friendship and support have been
instrumental in all that I have accomplished.*

Contents

Acknowledgments...xi

Introduction..1

1. Thought Awareness Training: *The First Step*.................9

2. Defining This Moment: *Interpretation Creates Experience*..29

3. Set Your Goals Using Accurate Data: *Stop Sabotaging Your Confidence*...39

4. Premeditated Procedures: *Escape the Drama*....................55

5. And Then What?: *A Mantra for Inner Peace*...................71

6. The "Perfect" Life: *Embracing the Experience of Constant Change*...83

7. You Have to Be There: *Seeing Opportunity in Moments of Struggle*...93

About the Author...101

Acknowledgments

I must thank my daughters, Margie and Melissa, for choosing me as their father in this life. They are two of my best friends and are amazing human beings.

Introduction

In my first book, *The Practicing Mind*, I wrote, "Everything in life worth achieving requires practice. In fact, life itself is nothing more than one long practice session, an endless effort of refining our motions." Here I would like to amend this quote to say that *everything* in life comes from practice. No matter how small or inconsequential we think it is, everything we do, from brushing our teeth to getting through a scary job interview, comes from practice, the deliberate repetition of an action with an awareness of what we want to achieve.

Learning to center your attention on the process of what you are doing instead of what you are trying to achieve, using the goal as a rudder instead of a reminder of what is left to be done, learning to work without judging your process: these are all simple shifts in perspective that completely transform the experience of going through your day.

This is the state of being fully engaged, the topic of the book you hold in your hands. We are only here in the now doing just what we are doing. We are absorbed in the process of what we are doing, not contemplating the future or the past and not judging how well or poorly we are doing. As long as we are working at that, we are successful. This is the type of subtle shift in perspective that I will discuss in *Fully Engaged* because it spells the difference between feeling successful and inspired and feeling like a failure.

There was a time in our culture when none of what I am discussing here would even be on anybody's radar. I am heartened by the fact that there is a global awakening taking place, an awareness that is moving to the forefront of our collective consciousness. As this ancient truth percolates up through the layers of discontent in our culture, a new paradigm for human potential is being born.

In the old paradigm, happiness, a sense of real contentment, is always outside us, a place we have to get to before we can experience it. Wherever we are in this moment we are incomplete, and the nectar that will quench that thirst lies outside ourselves and in some time frame other than the present moment. This feeling can burn within us our whole life, pushing us on in a state of exhaustion, like some poor soul stumbling through the desert trying to get to the water — which turns out to be a mirage.

Indeed, this feeling of incompleteness is what drives the marketing industry. Every day we are fed the message "Without this or that we cannot be happy." Because we are always connected in some form or another, whether it be through the internet, our smartphones, our TVs, or the radio, this feeling of incompleteness is easily nurtured because the people who wish to nurture it have constant access to us. Most of us blindly participate, even though in a moment of retrospection we can easily see how unproductive this cycle of "get more" has been in our lives. I call it the failure of SAS, Stuff Acquisition Syndrome. This mind-set pervades every area of our culture, especially the corporate world, an environment that promotes trends such as fewer individuals doing more work and constant multitasking, concepts that stem from the belief that we always need to get more, regardless of the cost.

Several years ago I was asked to do a working lunch at an investment firm in New York City. The CEO had read *The Practicing Mind* and liked it so much that he purchased copies for his employees and then asked me to visit for a day. I planned to take the trip up from Wilmington, Delaware, on a train that begins in Washington, DC, and has only a few stops before reaching New York. When I got on the train I could find only one seat, next to a businessman who had obviously boarded in Washington and was busy on his laptop. We didn't speak for the almost two-hour ride until we were about ten minutes out of New York, at which point he closed his laptop and started a conversation. He asked what brought me to New York, and when I mentioned that I had written a book and been invited to speak to a group, he asked me the title of the book. As I began to pull the book out of my briefcase he immediately recognized *The Practicing Mind* and asked, "Are you Tom Sterner?"

He said he couldn't believe he had missed an opportunity to have a conversation about the book. He went on to say that his company had come to the realization that they needed a new model for managing their employees. Their current model had passed the point of diminishing returns quite some time ago. Their employees were totally burned out and stressed out, and they were taking that stress home, creating more stress on that front, and then bringing that baggage back into the workplace the following day. It was a downward-spiraling cycle that was seriously impacting productivity and morale. *The Practicing Mind* was one of the books they were using as research in developing this new model.

I tell this story because it demonstrates the awakening that is happening on so many levels of our culture. The fact that by chance this gentleman had found himself sitting next to the author of a book his company was using as research in developing a new model for their work environment was an amusing coincidence. His acknowledgment that a change was truly needed for the survival of both the company and the employees, however, was a confirmation that the status quo is no longer effective in optimizing an individual's potential. It may have produced short-term increases in productivity, but the side effects of overall burnout, anxiety, and even underlying anger being experienced by employees is surely undermining their ability to perform consistently at high levels.

We are beginning to understand and accept the fact that personal power, real peace, and optimum productivity lie on a path that has always been here in front of us and is deceptively simple.

In my opinion this discovery began in sports decades ago. Because the field of sports is always pushing the threshold of performance and human potential, gaining a new edge, even if it requires going in an uncharted direction, is acceptable. Sports are also very individualized, which means performance levels are much more in the hands of each participant. Even in team sports, the team is made up of individuals who must each perform at their highest level in order for the team to be competitive and successful.

Sports also have the advantage of being able to divide performance into two areas: physical and mental. These two areas are divided only in theory, since in practice they are interrelated during each moment of execution. But for the sake of this discussion, let's say that once an athlete reaches a certain level of physical prowess, his ability to move past that falls on the mind. How disciplined the mind is, the mind's ability to focus, to quiet itself under stress, to eliminate destructive thoughts and create inspiring thoughts — all play a role in the level of an athlete's performance. Because of the importance of sports in our culture, we in the West have poured an enormous amount of money and research into understanding the fundamentals of human performance when it is operating at its highest level in sports.

When I first began to study sports psychology, more

than twenty-five years ago, I had already been studying Eastern thought for more than a decade. What immediately struck me was how in the West we were proving, through empirical science, what Eastern thought has been saying for thousands of years. So what does this mean? It means that we have come full circle. Modern studies in human psychology and ancient philosophical thought systems are in agreement, and we now understand how we perform at our highest level. We understand how to accomplish our goals with the least amount of effort in the least amount of time and without a sense of struggle. I have said many times that these truths have stood the test of time and that they have also stood the test of testing. Their precepts, meant to help us focus and unleash the power of the mind, have been practiced for centuries by spiritual traditions, and now through their applications in high-level sports, they have proved their value in helping us reach our full potential. More important, we need to integrate them into every area of our life. By doing so we will find ourselves immersed in the process of achieving our goals, regardless of what those goals happen to be. Whether our goal is to get through a job interview, deal with a difficult person, heal from an illness, or learn a golf swing, we can apply these truths, which bring us peace and contentment each moment, as well as increased productivity.

Initially, the idea of writing a follow-up to *The Practicing Mind* was intimidating and in some ways didn't seem necessary. After all, I had said all I had to say. What I wasn't prepared for was the overwhelmingly positive response to the ideas in the book. I have been contacted by an incredibly diverse audience of readers, from all over the world, ranging from adolescents to people well into their senior years. Their reasons for reading the book are equally as diverse.

Call it what you will — peace, productivity, profit, joy from being immersed in the *present moment*, from being in the *process* of achieving your goals, from *being fully engaged* in the experience of expanding your life — a new paradigm is taking us human beings to the next level. We had to exhaust our outward search in order to find that what we were looking for was always with us. We are now and have always been complete.

Helping groups and individuals integrate the mechanics of this new paradigm into every aspect of their lives is how I spend my days. I have found that regardless of the subject, from dating, to performing surgery, to investing, to learning an art form, to anything you can imagine, the mechanics apply equally well. Through the hundreds of interviews I have done, the Q&A sessions that have come at the end of speaking engagements, the workshops, and the one-on-one interactions I have had with coaching clients since the release of *The Practicing Mind*, I have gained an unexpected insight into some of the questions people ask after they read *The Practicing Mind*. That, combined with the number of people who have asked me, "Can you talk more about the concepts in your book and how I can apply them to my life?" has inspired me to write this book. It was my way of showing my gratitude. Let's get started.

Your mind will create thoughts
with or without your permission.
It can be your master or your servant.
Awareness offers you the opportunity
to make that choice.

CHAPTER 1

Thought Awareness Training

The First Step

To be fully engaged in an activity means to be present in this moment and in what you are doing right now. It also means to be completely content in that experience. There is no anxiousness about or sense of longing for the future, and there is no regret about the past. In our culture, living in this manner has become very foreign to us. Having an overactive mind, a mind that strongly resists being absorbed in this moment, a mind that can sometimes feel out of control, feels normal to us. Because of this we need to train ourselves to be aware of the thoughts our mind is producing at any moment, and we also need to learn what it feels like to experience a quieter mind. "How do I accomplish this?" is usually the first question asked of me in interviews. We are surrounded by so many distractions, so many temptations, all pulling us away from where we are and what we are doing. Some cultures are much more grounded in the here and now. However, as the pace of life has increased for us globally, and as much of the world has become more westernized, that perspective has dissolved in many cases and surrendered to a mind-set that is always reaching, always connected to a point in time other than the present. As for myself, I didn't need to be taught that mind-set; I was predisposed to having a butterfly brain when I was growing up. My mind was always generating thoughts, flitting around and changing directions, with me running after it.

As a child I had a vivid imagination and was very creative. Though that could be considered an asset, it can also have a distinct downside. When left unbridled, such a mind is very unfocused. It is always running off in different directions, exploring new adventures. Growing up, I could imagine anything, and anything I imagined I wanted to try. My mind was always in fifth gear, and a mind that operates like this is easily distracted and also very tiring, if its energy is not harnessed. This was the reason that I became so intense about each new endeavor and fairly quickly would burn up my initial enthusiasm to accomplish the new goal. At the same time that this mental fast-burn was going on, my mind would be offering up more ideas to explore, and those options would very quickly begin tugging at my attention. As a result, a silent competition would begin. I would expend enormous amounts of energy but complete very few goals.

In the end I would learn a little about many things, but I would feel like a failure. I might not have noticed this cycle at all, except that there was always this silent observer in me watching my behavior, listening to the promises I made to myself, watching me become distracted, hearing me make up excuses and repeat the same cycle over and over again. It was as if I were watching someone else. The "I," or at least who I thought "I" was, would feel disappointed and annoyed with me. The part of me I identified myself with had no self-confidence and felt like a failure. The observer, however, loved the part of me that it saw as possessing incredible amounts of creativity, a voracious appetite to learn new things, and an untapped potential to achieve any goal I could imagine, if I could only harness and focus my physical and mental energy.

My awareness of this observer who was separate from what I'll call the little me was what gradually propelled me out of this self-defeating cycle. It provided me with a sense that I could change how I was, how I processed life — if I could only figure out how. As time passed and my perspective became more biased toward the observer, I began to notice that my ability to achieve my goals, and perhaps more important, my experience both emotionally and mentally in each moment of achieving them, drastically changed from one of impatience and frustration into a relaxed peaceful sense of personal power. Ironically, my pursuit of the answer to that question may have been the first goal that I really completed. In reality, even when I thought I was a failure I was only in the process of learning what worked and what didn't. I was developing a practicing mind way before I chose to call it that, and self-awareness or "thought awareness training" is what made it all possible.

The key to becoming immersed in what I call "Present Moment Functioning," or PMF, is growing your connection to the observer within you, and you do this by what I'm calling "thought awareness training." You must learn to operate from the perspective that you are not your thoughts; you are the one who experiences your thoughts. Some thoughts you create intentionally, but most of us most of the time are the victims of the thoughts our mind creates without our permission. Without thought awareness you can't accomplish any real personal growth, and you have no authentic power. People often ask me, "How do I become more patient?" The first thing you have to do is become aware of when you are being impatient. That may sound obvious, but the fact is that most of the time when we are feeling impatient we are immersed in our impatience, not separate from it. When you experience an impatient thought as something separate that you can choose not to participate in instead of as something you are the puppet of, you have achieved the power of a conscious choice maker.

Here is a simple exercise that can open up a whole new world for you. I have used it many times with both large groups and individuals. Set a timer for two minutes. Sit comfortably in a chair, close your eyes, and stop thinking. After the timer goes off, open your eyes and take note of your experience.

When I ask people about their experience doing this,

the answer is always the same. They couldn't quiet their mind. Random thoughts just kept popping up out of nowhere. For many people this is an "aha" moment because it has never occurred to them that their mind would think without their permission, even if they were applying their will, *telling* it to stop. They also begin to realize that how they are feeling in any moment of the day has quite a lot to do with what their mind is thinking. Thought is the vehicle for stress, happiness, sadness, anger, and everything else we perceive as an experience. All these emotional experiences begin with a thought. We have a thought, and then our body reacts to our interpretation of that thought. In fact, I have often asked people at lectures I give, "If you didn't think, could you feel stress?" That's one for you to ponder. When we develop thought awareness, we give ourselves the gift of freedom of choice, of being a conscious choice maker. Virtually everything discussed in this book requires that you develop a strong connection to the observer within you, that you grow in your awareness of what your mind is doing behind the scenes all day long.

So how do we accomplish this? How do we become more aware of the thoughts our mind is producing all day long? We do this through only one exercise. That exercise, and I'm going to use a label here, is meditation. The practice of meditation teaches us to be an observer of and not a participant in our thoughts. It teaches us to notice what our mind is doing, to be more of a watcher of our thoughts. Through our practice we develop the ability to choose the thoughts that are productive and to lessen the ones that are not. Our thinking slows down and is much more purposeful. Our clarity increases, and our anxiety diminishes considerably.

I routinely hear many questions and comments about meditation: "How does one meditate?" "There are different forms of meditation; which should I use?" "How long do I need to meditate for it to be effective?" "I've tried to meditate, and I'm not very good at it. I can't stop my mind from thinking." So let's talk about what meditation is and what it isn't.

The first thing to understand is that, as I commented, the word *meditation* is a label for a process that accomplishes a number of things. If you're uncomfortable with that label for any reason, then call it "thought awareness training" because that is the crux of what we are accomplishing in becoming fully engaged. We are cultivating a connection with the observer, which is who we really are, not with the fear-based power-hungry ego with whom we often unconsciously identify ourselves. As we become more connected with this observer, we are growing our thought awareness, our ability to *watch* our thoughts instead of simply being immersed in them and reacting to whatever emotion or sensation they elicit.

Our mind tends to run around all day long, either visiting circumstances that have already happened or anticipating circumstances that may or may not happen in the future, even if that future is only moments away. It also operates in a constant state of judgment (which of course is a thought), and we experience the emotional content, which is the result of those judgments. This constant processing of internal dialogue, even though for most of us it happens without our awareness, is, to say the least, extremely draining.

It even affects our ability to sleep at night. I'm sure you have woken up in the middle of the night and experienced a brief period of mental stillness, of peacefulness, since your mind was not engaged in thinking. If you fall back asleep immediately, everything is fine. But if your mind gets just a little bit of traction and is able to reengage itself into its judgment process, all of a sudden the gears of internal dialogue start turning and that comforting pull back into slumber dissolves into restlessness: you begin worrying about something you wish you hadn't said, something you need to do, or something that is coming up in a day or two that you don't want to deal with.

The mind doesn't like the present moment — or at least it doesn't like being instructed to *be* in the present moment. It thinks there's nothing for it to do there. It loves to problem solve. And if you don't give it a problem to solve, it will go looking for one. That is its nature, and it's not always a bad thing. In fact, it's why we live in heated homes instead of in caves, shivering. We just need to be aware of what our mind is up to, and more important, to be *in charge* of what it is up to. A self-propelled riding lawn mower is a great tool and certainly makes cutting the front lawn easier than it would be with a pair of scissors. However, its usefulness becomes questionable if we are not guiding it but are instead sitting on our front step talking on our cell phone while it is running through our flower bed and chasing the neighbor's cat. In that case, instead of serving us, it is creating problems for us.

A daily practice of meditation, of thought awareness training, grows our innate ability to be aware of what our mind is doing, and through strengthening our will, it grows our ability to use our mind's energy to serve us in ways we can't even imagine. What's interesting about this process is that you don't have to try to grow your thought awareness. It happens on its own. In fact, you cannot stop it from happening. It's really quite subtle. At first, you don't realize that your awareness is growing. But gradually you begin to notice that life doesn't bother you as much anymore. Circumstances that used to push your buttons begin to lose their effect on you. You see them coming and either effortlessly deflect them or just step aside and let them go past. This happens because you are no longer a puppet of your thoughts but instead are an objective observer of them.

At the same time, your productivity begins to increase drastically because all your energy is going into whatever you are doing right now, from washing the dishes to supporting a loved one through a difficult situation. The reason for this is that you have access to your full consciousness. You have clarity of thought and focus. Your ability to make decisions is significantly enhanced, and it could even be said that your life feels more inspired. Difficult situations are also much less fatiguing because you aren't in a constant state of judging.

One time I was asked to do an evening lecture in a town I was unfamiliar with, about fifty miles from my home. It was during the winter so I wouldn't have the advantage of daylight in finding the location. I had a general idea of how to get there using the interstate, but once I got off the interstate, everything would be unfamiliar. I had GPS, but as we know, they're not infallible, and this happened to be one of those times when the device completely let me down. I found myself lost in the dark, running late, with a GPS that kept trying to take me to a small diner instead of to where the event was being held. Because it was cold and dark, there was no one walking around that I could ask. I knew I was keeping people waiting. I also had the normal anxiousness that comes from having to do a presentation in front of an unfamiliar group. The one phone number that I had was the office number of a liaison that I had worked with in setting the whole thing up, but that person was already at the event.

This could have been a panic situation. However, because of my daily meditation practice, I found that I was connected to my inner observer, and that observer was calmly looking at my options. The thoughts of panic were there just waiting for a chance to be expressed, but they had very little influence over me. I was aware of their presence, but they stayed in the background. I reminded myself just to remain present in the situation and to let each moment unfold however it did. This is one of the key benefits of a daily meditation practice. As it teaches you to notice your thoughts, it also gives you the mental strength to shut off or at least hold at bay the thoughts that are not serving you in a particular situation. Feeling calm and inwardly quiet allowed me to intuitively notice a feeling that I should try traveling down a particular street, even though it was so dark I couldn't read any of the signs. I had turned the GPS off at this point because it was useless. After traveling down the street for about a block, off to the left I saw the building where the event was being held. From then on it was an effortless evening. My training had transformed a situation that could have been filled with anxiety into one in which I felt in control the entire time.

There is another vital reason for undertaking a thought awareness practice. Adapting to the hyper pace of life in our culture is stealing away our ability to focus, to pay attention for any length of time. As discussed, our lives are all moving at a faster and faster pace. Is there anyone who feels there's enough time in the day to get everything done? I think most of us will agree that the demands on our time and energy are unreasonable, yet we all participate in a lifestyle that is burning us out. This is true not just for adults but for children, too. We keep trying to squeeze a little more performance, a little more achievement, a little more productivity into each day. What studies have shown is that in order to accomplish this, our brains have had to adapt. Basically, we are asking our brains to evolve to handle this high pace of living, and they are obliging us. Our lifestyle effectively increases our mind's activity. It ramps up our internal dialogue considerably as our mind struggles to solve all the situations it is faced with in a day.

Meditation, or thought awareness, counters this process by slowing our mind down, pulling it into the present, and thinning out thoughts that are not relevant to this moment. In short, a meditative thought awareness practice slows your mind down, which gives you focused clarity of thought. Over time the focused clarity of thought gained from meditating becomes an on-demand skill you possess, and you gain back so much energy lost on redundant and unproductive thinking.

This is not the first time in history that our brains have had to shift up a gear to keep pace. Think back to when the printing press was first invented. Up until that point very few people could read, mostly because there was nothing for them to read. When books became more available, literacy became more widespread. But how would our brains have handled that? We take it for granted when we read a sentence in a book that our mind interprets all the letters and words. We also take it for granted that when those words are strung together they create a sentence that creates a picture in our mind when we read it. But it wasn't always so simple. Our brains had to evolve and learn to do that to help us keep pace with the major paradigm shift that came as a result of the printing press.

Because our brains are marvelous instruments, they are, in fact, evolving to work at higher speeds. The downside is that, as studies show, we are losing our ability to slow our mind down, to focus it on one thing at a time. Like a muscle that is no longer being used, this faculty of our brain is atrophying. This is not because our brains cannot continue to do this; it's because we are not *asking* them to. One of my daughters teaches early childhood education, and we have had numerous discussions about the short attention span and impatience being documented in children today. Many educators and psychologists feel that meditation should be part of the school curriculum, and I couldn't agree more.

I once did a presentation for high school students, and we started off with the two-minute exercise mentioned earlier. Their reaction to the exercise was nothing short of amazing. Not only were they caught completely off guard at how active their mind was and how little control they had over it, but they were also inspired to pursue meditation. Even in those two minutes they could feel the potential for greater focus and also for the sense of relief that comes from a less active mind. One of the young women in the class began meditating daily. Later I received a phone call from her mother, who told me how the practice had transformed her daughter's ability to focus and perform in school. This young student offered to do a testimonial video for other high school students, telling them how much meditating had helped her. Imagine what students could do if this training were started early in their school years.

Now that we've established some good background, let's get back to our questions. How does one meditate or practice thought awareness training? If you've ever been curious about meditation, you may have found that there are numerous forms, but in my opinion they boil down to three general systems: guided meditation; breath-based meditation; and phrase-based, or mantra-based, meditation. In the context of becoming fully engaged I don't feel guided meditations are particularly useful. Though they have many wonderful applications, and at times I use them myself, they have the shortcoming of requiring you to *think*. You are being guided to visualize through spoken word, and this requires you to process instructions, which is the opposite of what we are trying to achieve here. We want a still mind, or at least one that is as still as we can manage. We want to disengage from the thought process and simply observe the thinking that is going on normally without our objective perspective. Because of this I favor either breath-based or phrase-based meditation.

Either of these two systems is very effective for accomplishing our goal. You also may wish to experiment back and forth between the two styles to see which one resonates with you more. The mechanics for both are deceptively simple. In a breath-based meditation you assume a comfortable position so that you will not be distracted by any aches or pains. You want to be focused internally. This becomes more difficult when your foot goes to sleep or your ankle starts to throb. It should also be noted this kind of discomfort gives rise to thoughts, because you have to be thinking in order to notice that your foot is going to sleep.

You could lie down to meditate, but you may find that it's hard not to fall asleep, which is why I generally stay away from that position. The more common positions are sitting comfortably in a chair with your spine erect (a hunched-over position breeds drowsiness as you become more relaxed during the meditation); some people prefer a kneeling position. You can kneel on a cushion and then place a pillow between the backs of your thighs and your calf muscles. This keeps you from putting stress on your knees and also from sitting on your heels, which can become uncomfortable. One advantage of kneeling is that it forces your spine into a very upright position and also promotes keeping your head level, which you want to do in both seated and kneeling positions.

You could also sit in a cross-legged posture, a position we are all familiar with from childhood (when it was sometimes called "criss-cross applesauce"). In a soft chair with armrests, this position can be quite comfortable. The same chair can also work well if you prefer to have your feet flat on the floor. If you are particularly flexible, you could assume the full-lotus position, in which you sit cross-legged, but with your feet resting on opposite thighs. Not many adults can manage a full-lotus position, and if you can, you have probably been meditating for years! You can do both the cross-legged and the full-lotus posture on a cushion on the floor; just note that you will need to work more diligently at keeping your spine as erect as possible since you will not have the back of the chair to support you.

To do a breath-based meditation, simply sit or kneel and begin watching your body breathe. The temptation is for the mind to get involved and to try to control your breathing, but you want to resist this and just quietly watch your body breathe. Obviously, our bodies don't need our conscious instruction to breathe, or we would all be in trouble. In a phrase-based meditation you choose a simple phrase to repeat. For our purposes the phrase is probably best kept to three words or fewer and should be something that comforts you such as "I am still" or "I am quiet." Some people may find a phrase-based system a little easier because it gives the mind one thought to focus on, discouraging it from randomly generating multitudes of other thoughts.

That's it. As I've said, the mechanics are deceptively simple. But oh, if only it were just that simple. Here is what you will most likely experience very early in your practice: For maybe the first sixty seconds your practice will have your full attention, and it will seem pretty effortless. But at some point you will wake up to the fact that you are no longer watching your breath or repeating your mantra. Your mind has run off and is now visiting some unrelated situation. It could be something you're worried about, something you're looking forward to doing, or something you have to get done. Your mind can even come up with a very creative idea that you need to include in the book you are writing, making you feel you need to stop meditating so you can write it down before you forget it. It is very clever that way. One thing you can be sure of: your mind will not be where you are and focused on what you are doing. It has a very short attention span, much like a toddler in a toy store. It wants to run off in all different directions, checking things out. It wants to generate thoughts, to solve problems, to come up with ideas, and to judge.

Your mind serves a very valuable purpose, but even so, no matter how much it insists on being so, it should not be the master. When you realize that your mind has tricked you into allowing it to run off, simply bring it back to the present moment and to the task at hand. That is the practice in its entirety. It's quite amazing, when you consider the incredible power this simple activity gives you.

When you begin a meditation practice and find that you struggle to stop thinking, it is easy to interpret that as an indication that you are not good at meditating, but this is not the case. A quiet mind is the goal and should serve as a rudder to steer your efforts, not as an indicator of what you have not yet accomplished. That perspective puts you in a place of struggle. It could be said that the practice of meditation, of thought awareness training, is the *repetitive* action of catching the mind as it runs off with the *intention* of bringing it back to the task of watching your breath or repeating your phrase. As long as you are doing that, you are staying present and you are succeeding. It doesn't matter how many times your mind runs off. You will find that some days your mind is quieter and less prone to wandering. Other days you may feel that you can't focus it for more than a few seconds. This is normal and all part of the experience.

I am always amused when people interpret the fact that they are chasing their mind all the time as an indicator that they are not good at meditation. What they are missing, and this is very significant, is that they wouldn't be chasing their mind and bringing it back to task if they weren't *noticing* that their mind was running off! I have commented many times that what many people interpret as a bad meditation is really a good one, if not a great one, because they are getting many opportunities to pull their mind back. In my opinion the real juice of meditating is the raising of your thought awareness in that microsecond when you wake up and catch your mind. This is when you are expanding. This is when the observer is growing and your will is strengthening. Your will is your highest intention for yourself, the most desired action you would execute in any circumstance. It allows us to resist everything from anger to that second (or maybe third) slice of pizza. It is the resolve that makes us leave the couch and take a walk, and the simple act of meditating nurtures its strength and its availability to us when we need it most.

Understand that we never master this practice, in the normal sense of the word. We don't achieve a perfectly quiet mind 100 percent of the time; nobody does. Again, the quiet mind serves as the rudder to steer our effort. The perfect practice is just doing it. It's like physical exercise. We never reach a point when we say, "Well, I finally made it. I have mastered exercising. My body no longer needs this activity." Exercise is a necessary ingredient of a healthy lifestyle. Thought awareness training is as well.

How long do we need to sit (or kneel) in meditation? Not as long as you might think. Ten to fifteen minutes in the morning and perhaps again later in the day or evening is a great place to start. It's best to start with shorter times that you know you can commit to. The experience of feeling your mind slow down, particularly in our hyper culture, is so inviting that it won't take long before you start to look forward to these quiet, internally focused moments. As you progress, you will probably want to commit to longer periods, of perhaps thirty minutes or maybe even more.

I said that no one ever achieves a perfectly quiet mind 100 percent of the time, but I didn't say we never achieve a quiet mind. Through faithful practice, you will begin to experience more and more times when your mind stops fighting you and just drops into idle mode. The paradox here is that the minute you begin to think, "Hey, I'm not thinking anymore," you have just started to think again. But you will have times when you are simply aware of how still your mind is. The experience is beyond words. Just know that it is a peaceful and rejuvenating place to be.

We've been discussing the mental and emotional benefits of a thought awareness practice, but what about the many physical benefits? Here are just a few. Meditating will slow down your heart rate, it will slow your breathing rate, it will normalize your blood pressure, and it will help your mind age at a slower rate. It's also free, it has no potential side effects, and you don't need any special equipment to do it.

It is important to go into this with the understanding that once you start your practice there will be days, maybe even several in a row, when you will miss a session.

It happens to all of us. When that happens, remember, there is no judgment. Simply make your observation that you have fallen off the wagon of your practice and correct by getting back on. Just as in the practice itself when you catch your mind and direct it back to the task, you do the same with dropping back into your practice. You notice that you have missed a few sessions and you correct; that's all. Negative self-commentary has no place in this. Just noticing your actions and pulling yourself back into your practice is success. So give yourself a present — the present moment.

*As awareness of your thoughts increases,
the opportunity to choose how you
experience this moment also increases.*

CHAPTER 2

Defining This Moment

Interpretation Creates Experience

Thought awareness training is essential for becoming more fully engaged and bringing the practicing mind into your life. The mechanics are few and easy to understand. This training requires the process of practice, which is an awareness of what you are trying to accomplish, repetition of specific mechanics necessary for that accomplishment, present-moment attention to your effort, and conscious intention to steer your efforts. This cycle continually refines itself. It's like putting a dull pencil in a pencil sharpener. As you turn the handle or activate the motor, the blades repeatedly rotate around the pencil, honing it to a focused point.

But another aspect of this process, if not taken into account, can quickly erode the intensity and enthusiasm of your drive. That aspect is simply your interpretation of this moment. How do you interpret the experience of what you are doing right now? Any time we develop a new skill, we begin at a place that we will call "no skill." Moving along the path of mastery is like moving along a time line representing "increments of skill expansion." I call it this because anything past "no skill" *is* some level of skill. If you start with nothing, anything you add to that becomes something. Most of the time mastering a skill is not a place that you get to; it is an ever-expanding awareness and understanding of what is possible in the skill itself and of how to execute it more effortlessly.

When you have your first child, as a parent you are starting from a point of no skill. You don't know how to change a diaper, how to hold a newborn, how to feed her, how much and when to feed her, and so on. Yet very quickly you begin to develop the skills of a good parent. As your child grows you are constantly faced with new situations. You experience the "terrible twos," the first day at school, the teenage driver, and sending your child off to college. All these fall along the path of mastering parenthood. Just as I discussed in *The Practicing Mind*, you use the DOC principle: you Do, you Observe, and you Correct over and over again, constantly refining your actions.

The process is the same for everything, whether you are learning a physical skill such as playing golf or a musical instrument or a more abstract nonphysical skill such as dealing with a difficult person, handling stressful situations, or switching careers. Many of the people I work with as a business or life coach are entrepreneurs. They have left corporate jobs and moved on to owning their own businesses. They may have accumulated elements of wisdom and experience that help guide them along the time line, but they are still entrepreneurs for the first time in their life, starting from a place of no skill and immediately moving away from that point on the time line of skill development.

We call this moving forward along the time line "learning." Learning in itself is a neutral value, with no good or bad nature to it. *We* decide how we will experience the process of learning, that is, we interpret it; we make judgments about it. But when we are fully engaged in the process of learning something, when we are fully in the moment, we do not experience judgment or the corresponding emotions. Judgments happen *outside* the process.

When I was in college I had to take an accounting course. I absolutely hated accounting. From a right-brained person's perspective, math was not fun, and staring at debit and credit columns made it even worse. I dreaded the class and struggled to get even a C. However, the person sitting next to me in class, who was a friend of mine, lived for this class. We would be walking to the class and he would say, "What day is this? Oh, it's a Wednesday. Great! We have an accounting lab today, so it's two hours instead of just one." The class was the highlight of his day. I jokingly told him he needed to reevaluate his life, but this story demonstrates a point. The accounting, and the process of learning it, was neither good nor bad; it was just accounting. My friend and I interpreted that class differently, and consequently our experience of it was quite different.

We could easily say that some situations are, in fact, difficult. We have sayings such as "that was a hard lesson to learn." But I have not found that interpretation to be consistent from one person to the next. One evening I was watching a program about an investor who had started a business and lost 400 million dollars in the venture. He said, "It looked like a good investment, but it turned out to be problematic. We'll make it up on the next one. I learned a lot from the venture." His response was very nonchalant, but another person's might very well have been hysterical. It's all relative.

Your interpretation of this moment determines your experience of it, and it also determines your ability to perform at your best. One time I was conducting a golf clinic for high school and college golfers. One of the best golfers in the room, a high schooler who had won the club championship at this country club, beating out even the best adult players, asked me an interesting question. "I am winning a tournament, I'm on the eighteenth hole, and either I can go directly at the green, which means I will have to carry water, or I can play safe and go farther left and take the water out of play. Should I take the risk? If I carry the water, I will be on the green in two and have a very good chance at a birdie and gain the safety margin of one stroke. If I play it safe and go to the left, taking the water out of play, I will effectively add one more stroke to the hole, and my chances of birdieing the hole will be greatly diminished." This is a common risk-versus-reward scenario built into the design of each golf hole. Do I take the safe path, which is easier, or do I take the more difficult path to reap the reward? The risk is that if I execute the shot successfully, I am rewarded with a good chance for a lower score. However, if I fail, then I will most likely suffer the consequence of increasing my score on the hole. For example, in this scenario if he were to take the risk, mis-hit the ball, and come up short in the water, he would be penalized a stroke on the hole and still have to hit another shot to get to the green.

I replied that a number of factors were involved in his decision, not the least of which was how far behind him his nearest competitor was in the score and how many holes that person had left to play. He would need to consider that because if the other player was only one stroke behind him but still had several holes to play, that player would have numerous opportunities to beat his score. That scenario could weigh heavily on his decision. But aside from that, I told him that the most significant thing that would impact his decision was using the word *risk*, when he asked, "Should I take the risk?"

He looked confused, so I gave him a hypothetical distance of 162 yards that he had to hit the ball to carry it over the water and land it on the green. He responded that that would be an easy seven iron for him. I told him that even though the club and the distance didn't scare him, he had still made it into a difficult shot by his interpretation of it being a risk. I told him that if I put him on the fairway 162 yards from his target, he would probably say to himself, "This is a no-brainer," and put an easy swing on the ball.

He had unknowingly brought some very influential factors into the same shot, and now his experience of hitting a "no-brainer" was filled with anxiety and uncertainty, both of which were going to affect his ability to execute. His interpretation of the situation was telling his brain to "pull out the swing I use when I feel nervous and come from a place of 'I hope I don't mess this up because the tournament is riding on it.'" The physical swing was one he had proven his ability to execute thousands of times, and yet his interpretation of the situation was going to affect his ability to be successful. You might be saying, "That's true, but it was still a riskier shot because of the possible consequences of not executing it correctly." My response to that is of course it is, but coming from that perspective greatly reduces his ability to succeed. We're just talking about a hypothetical golf swing here, but in other areas of life if you could choose how to interpret a situation (and you can if you are aware of your thoughts), which interpretation would you choose? Surrendering to a perspective of "I just can't help the way I feel" is not only disempowering but untrue.

I have always been fascinated by how our interpretation of a situation can impact our experience so drastically. A common example used to demonstrate this is the walking-the-board analogy. Take a board that is twelve inches wide by twenty feet long. Lay it on the ground and ask someone to walk the board. He will do it with perfect balance and effortless ease. His brain has no trouble instructing his body to do what it interprets as a simple task.

Now take that same board and hang it fifty feet in the air between the rooftops of two buildings, and ask the same person to walk the board. It becomes an extremely frightful and difficult task. Though the consequences of falling off the board are more serious, the actual task is physically no different. The brain issues the same set of instructions to the body. The interpretation of the situation is what creates the fear and thus the inability to perform.

Some people might say that you can't get past this; it is human nature. But every day this is proved untrue. Firefighters run into burning buildings to save people. Rescuers of all types learn, through practiced procedures, how to squelch the knee-jerk interpretation of a very dangerous situation so that they are able to perform the necessary tasks. When I trained to be a pilot, the repetition of various procedures allowed me to interpret a potentially life-threatening situation properly so that I could be calm, focused, and effective in that moment.

Not only does our interpretation of the moment determine whether we can perform at our best (or even at all), but also, especially in less crucial activities, it can be instrumental in determining whether we become bored, impatient, or frustrated. It either creates or diminishes the energy we need to sustain our effort. Try to *notice* your interpretation of any given moment during the day. The opportunities to do that will constantly increase as you become more connected to the observer and more aware of your thoughts. You will find yourself more actively conscious during your day and more empowered with the privilege of choice.

After you give yourself the choice, how can you best use the opportunity? Situations that you find comfortable and pleasant don't require you to change your interpretation of them. What we are looking at here are situations that you find stressful or generally unpleasant. When you're feeling bored or impatient, that's a good indication that you are not fully present in the activity. You may be physically present, but mentally you are someplace else. Just as you do in your meditation practice, work at pulling your focus back into what you are doing in this moment. This can be challenging when you feel very distracted. In moments like these it is good to remind yourself that this is an opportunity. When something feels difficult it is because you are up against the threshold of your ability. That means that in this moment you are pushing through a barrier.

The reason for engaging in practices such as meditation, in which we increase our ability to know our thoughts and to control them, is so that we can increase our ability to be in control of what we experience. If I were to ask you if you'd like to be in total control of yourself in every situation, I'm sure you would say that absolutely, you would. Who wouldn't want to be? You can't get better at an activity unless you are up against the threshold of your ability. That is when you have the opportunity to move forward, even if it's only a small amount. Changing your interpretation of how you experience whatever difficulty you are facing can help revitalize your focus and keep you inspired.

Interpreting a situation as stressful usually has its roots in a feeling of not being in control. In those situations either we don't know what to do or we get pulled into our emotions, anticipating possible outcomes. The most powerful and dependable way of changing your experience of these situations is with a premeditated procedure. Creating a plan for how to deal with stressful situations and people *before* you're actually confronted by them can drastically change how you experience those situations. We'll cover this in detail a little further on.

Your goals should inspire you,
not serve as a reminder of what you have
left to accomplish. Understanding all that is
involved in reaching your goals frees you to
experience the joy of achieving them.

CHAPTER 3

Set Your Goals Using Accurate Data

Stop Sabotaging Your Confidence

How you interpret your experience in this moment is affected considerably by how you set your goals. If you create goals with either inaccurate or insufficient information regarding what is involved in accomplishing them, you may unknowingly put yourself in a position of experiencing frustration and failure, even though you may be progressing at an incredible rate. Because we become so attached to the moment when we achieve our goals, we generally underthink all that is involved in the process of achieving them. If we remain unaware of this tendency, it is all too easy to sabotage our sense of confidence in our ability to see the process through. I speak from experience.

The current version of *The Practicing Mind* was published in April 2012, but I originally wrote the book in the mid-1990s. I wrote it over a five-week period, working several hours each morning after dropping my daughters off at preschool. Initially I thought the hard part was behind me, but I was wrong.

When I began writing, I had already done considerable research about the publishing process and concluded that I probably couldn't get into a publishing company without an agent, and getting an agent without being a published author was akin to needing to have credit before getting your first bank loan. Self-publishing seemed to be my only reasonable option, and it didn't intimidate me in the least. It was just another adventure for me to experience, another skill to develop.

I first made a short list of what I needed to accomplish. The book needed to be edited, a process I had never experienced. I would go through that "vale of tears" later on. I needed a cover design, a printer, and a means of distribution. Finding a printer was pretty straightforward research, and distribution would be limited to Amazon and a website. Coming up with a cover design required not just artistic skill but knowledge about what would encourage a person to pick up the book. I had done quite a bit of graphic arts work, so I didn't feel I would be short on ideas, but I did feel I needed to hand the real artwork over to a professional.

The first wall I ran into had little to do with the book itself. I had a very successful service business that had taken me many years to build. I was a high-level concert piano technician and remanufacturer. I was contracted to fully restore large grand pianos back to factory-new condition (many times providing custom modifications), and I also prepared the instruments for artists of every genre, both in concert halls and at outdoor venues. I was moving through four states regularly and working seven days a week. From a business perspective this demand for my skills was wonderful, but with regards to getting my book out on the market it presented a real problem. I simply couldn't find the time I needed to learn how to publish a book and get all the details taken care of. It was all I could do to keep up with the work I had scheduled and to spend time with my family. As a result the book lived quietly as a Word document on my computer for almost ten years.

It wasn't that I had stopped trying to achieve my goal of publishing the book. It was more a matter of figuring out what needed to change in my life, and how to change it, so that I could see the project through. I realized that the first problem I had to solve was the fact that I had no control over my schedule. I was on the run from about 6:30 in the morning until as late as midnight. In retrospect, the diversity of situations I encountered and the demands for my skills on any given day were almost comical. My first call of the day could be working on a hundred-year-old piano, trying to get every key to at least make a sound when it was pressed so that a new student could practice her weekly lesson. Two hours later, as a chief concert piano technician, I could be working on a very expensive concert Steinway and preparing that instrument to produce the most subtle nuance of sound beneath the fingers of a legendary concert piano soloist.

It was clear that if I was ever going to have the opportunity to work toward my goal, I was going to have to get better control of my time. I needed to free up dependable blocks of time that would allow me to execute a plan for getting the book published and distributed. My brilliant idea was to take on full-scale piano remanufacturing. Initially this seemed like the perfect solution, but in fact it ended up compounding the problem. Up until that point I had done limited restoration work out of my house. To do full-scale restorations I would need space in a commercial facility. That, of course, would cost money and create a bigger financial nut for me to crack every month, but the increased income from high-level restoration work would certainly cover that — or so I thought. My thinking at the time was that shop work had the advantage of being flexible. Unlike a day of service on the road, which required me to be at one location at 8:00 AM, another location twenty miles away at 9:30, and so forth, on a shop day I could first work for several hours in my home office, setting up my publishing company, and then go to the shop and put in work time. I still had concert obligations, but because I had my own keys to the concert hall I could often prepare the instrument when it suited my schedule. Many times I went into the concert hall at 5:00 AM, set up the instrument, and then came back for the concert that evening to be on hand if necessary.

On paper it seemed to be a well-thought-out plan. I needed the income that the business would produce to publish and market the book. Letting go of some of the door-to-door work to gain several flexible days a week without losing, and maybe even gaining, income seemed like a win-win situation. The first indicator that maybe this wasn't the slickest deal came when I began the process of finding a facility and getting all the machinery set up. It was an immense undertaking and backbreaking work that took weeks out of my schedule. I was hemorrhaging money setting things up, and I was losing money by taking myself off the street — never a good combination.

After I had the shop set up, the next "oh dear" I experienced was when I let my clients know that I would be available to take on full remanufacturing work. It took me about six weeks to book more than two years of work, and that never let up. I couldn't very well turn work away, because the shop facility itself was costing quite a bit of money to operate. I could keep going, but I think you get the point. What I thought was a great idea and a solution to my problem had instead created more commitments and less time than I had had when I was doing just outside service work. I did have more money coming in the door, but I also had way more money going out. In addition, because both ends of the business had continued to grow, instead of gaining hours to work on my publishing company I was working longer hours, trying to keep up with all the demands. It really reached a level of absurdity. There were days when I left the house at 5:00 AM, set up a concert piano, drove back home and got my daughters to school, then left to do my work, came home and had dinner with the family, went back over to the shop and worked until almost midnight, after which I would come home and fall into bed.

I finally decided that if I was ever going to get *The Practicing Mind* out there I was going to have to walk away from everything and dedicate myself to nothing else. I was going to have to sell the two business properties I had purchased several years earlier, sell off tens of thousands of dollars in commercial machinery and a client base that had taken me thirty years to build, and jump off a cliff, all the while assuming I would figure out how to fly before I hit bottom. So in 2005 I did just that. Some thought it was a gutsy move, with two daughters who would be in college in just a few years. Others probably thought I was having a midlife crisis: "You're going to do what? You're going to sell everything you've worked for since you were in college, write a self-help book, and make a new career? Sounds like a crash-and-burn story to me."

I saw things from a different perspective, and I still felt fully engaged and enthusiastic about the whole process. I wanted to spend the second half of my life serving and connecting with people on a much larger scale. It was also time for a change. There really wasn't much room left in my career to grow. I had been all over the country studying with different people. I had met many of the finest musicians and conductors of our time, and I felt as if I needed to expand as a person and use some of the other talents I felt I possessed. So I pulled the trigger.

Even though I wasn't consciously aware of it, I was beginning to learn that I had set a goal with very inaccurate data in terms of what was realistically involved in accomplishing it and how long the process should take. Though I didn't know it at the time, I had quite a bit more coming down the road to make sure I learned this lesson thoroughly. Getting rid of everything went smoothly. I was cash rich and had all the time in the world to set up a publishing company and live my dream. Now that I was in a position to devote all my energy to accomplishing my goal, I *assumed* that my problems were behind me. I would get the book edited (how long could that take? It was already written), get a cover design, get an ISBN number and a bar code, have a website built, put the book on Amazon, and through the vastness of the internet connect with people all over the world, sell unimaginable numbers of copies, and live happily ever after. It wasn't that I had the sequence of events incorrect. It was my time frame that was so far off the mark.

During the editing process I felt as though I were being asked to rewrite the book. My editor would kindly say, "I don't know what you mean here." I would say, "What's not to understand? It seems perfectly clear to me." To which she would respond, "That's because you wrote it. You already understand it. But if your readers don't understand what you are trying to teach them, then there really isn't much point to the book, is there?" And so it went for hours and hours. At times it felt as if I were birthing an elephant. But it really helped me become clear about what I was trying to say. While that was going on, I was working on the cover design with a professional artist and also with a web designer. As soon as the final, edited manuscript was completed and the book went out for printing, I began production work on the audio version in my recording studio.

In January 2006 a truck pulled up in front of my house and unloaded a thousand copies of *The Practicing Mind*. It was very exciting. I ripped into one of the boxes to pull out a copy and thought, "I've made it." The website went live shortly after that, Amazon was stocked, and the audiobook version was ready for sale. It was time to sit back and make money. But that didn't happen. Nobody knew who I was, and nobody knew about the book. Because I wasn't bringing in any cash, I could feel the stress mounting. Should I spend a lot of money on promotion? What if it doesn't work? Then I'm just out of the money and no better off.

The book did begin to sell, but as with so many other self-published titles, the sales were extremely modest. A few copies would go out the door from the website, and each month there would be some sales on Amazon. But the sales did not exactly instill confidence in the choice I had made. Now it was becoming increasingly difficult for me to stay fully engaged in the whole process. I was losing confidence in my dream. It wasn't that I hadn't covered a lot of ground. In fact, what I had accomplished was amazing, but it didn't feel that way. Inside I was questioning myself continually, and I didn't feel I could share that with those around me. I didn't need to hear "I told you so" on top of everything else. I also didn't feel I could change direction; I was in it up to my neck. I had spent untold hours and dollars getting to where I was. I couldn't just walk away, and the truth is, I didn't want to.

Money aside, I was doing exactly what I wanted to do, continually researching a subject that had changed my life in such a positive way and using my creativity to help other people. In fact, what was allowing me to cope and keep moving forward was everything that I had written about in the book itself. What I hadn't realized at that point was that most of my anxiety stemmed from my initial lack of information about how long this whole process could or should take. My lack of understanding was actively disengaging me from the process of accomplishing my goal. It was tugging at my confidence and whispering doubts in my ears, as I tried my best to maintain focus and confidence.

In time the book began to take hold, and sales began to increase dramatically. It was number one in stress management on Amazon twice. But that didn't take months. It took years. I eventually began to look at it as "the little book that thought it could." I realized that the whole thing just needed more time to develop, and yet the financial struggles that were the by-product of that time were quite difficult. At one point I put myself back out on the job market and did production work for other people in my studio. I even did a short stint as a roadie at the concert hall where I used to be at the top of the food chain. It was not an easy place to be at fifty-two years old: finding myself surrounded by twentysomethings at two o'clock in the morning, pushing crates up into a semi so the artist who had performed that night could get to the next town. I had always been self-employed because I learned growing up that I wanted to be in charge of my destiny, and I didn't enjoy being yelled at by someone simply because they were my superior and could get away with it. But I did what I had to do to give my dream the time it needed to mature. It all came around.

The life of *The Practicing Mind* has truly been amazing, and it has continued its upward trend. I have met people from all over the world, connected with all kinds of folks through email and phone calls, been on television and been interviewed on some pretty big radio shows. When people say to me that it must be wonderful "to be where I am," I tell them, "It's been a ten-year overnight success." But if I were more honest, I would admit that my experience of the journey could have been quite a bit different if I had been much clearer at the outset.

I am not alone in this. Most of us, when we are setting goals, disempower ourselves at the get-go by investing little or no effort into understanding a realistic time frame for accomplishing those goals. Instead we make an unconscious and uninformed assumption about what the time frame should be. We then begin judging our progress based on where we are in relationship to that time frame. This can very quickly erode our confidence in our ability to achieve the goal, even when in reality we may be excelling in the process. It blinds us to the progress we have made and sabotages our ability to remain fully engaged in our effort.

I have seen this in myself, though much less frequently now, and I have seen it in most everyone that I work with. As a further example, I once worked with someone who, like me, had changed careers in midlife. She wanted to become a visual artist. When she left her corporate job, she began studying what she thought she needed to know in order to be successful in her new endeavor. When we first began talking, it became clear that she was struggling with what she perceived as a lack of progress. When I asked her where the struggle was coming from, she responded that she had been working at her new project for six months and felt that she wasn't as good as she should be. Looking for a point of relativity, I asked her, "How good should you be, then?" There was silence on the other end of the phone, and eventually she said, "You know, I really don't know." Without thinking I asked her, "If you don't know how good you should be after six months of effort, how do you know you're not *better* than you should be?" Again there was silence, followed by, "I guess I don't know that, either. I hadn't thought of it that way." So I asked, "If you had had the skills you have now six months ago, would you have felt you were pretty good?" Her response was quick and certain: that she absolutely would have. I commented that perhaps the problem wasn't that she wasn't improving and moving forward; it was that her perception of what "good" means and her understanding of how good she could get was constantly evolving. Wasn't that always going to be the case? When you adopt this perspective, your experience of the moment changes drastically, even though it can be a very subtle shift.

I believe our tendency to fall into this trap comes from our impatience to reach the goal, from our attachment to the moment when we achieve it. This is a misuse of the goal itself because it pulls us out of the process of achieving and creates a sense of struggle. Instead of nurturing our confidence in our ability to reach our goal, it fosters a sense of failure and takes away from our efforts. We will discuss this in detail in chapter 5.

An extreme example of this would be to say, "I would like to lose thirty pounds. That should take three weeks." Of course this sounds ridiculous but only because it falls into the arena of common knowledge. But in many endeavors, such as creating a publishing business, writing a book, and having it become successful, we participate in the same behavior. I certainly did. Actually, I was not only naive about how long it would take *The Practicing Mind* to get up to speed; I was equally naive as to how many people it could and has reached. If I had known that right from the beginning, or even just been aware of the possibilities, my ability to stay fully engaged in the process and my experience of the process would have been completely different.

Going back to the weight-loss example, even if you begin a very healthy diet and a sensible exercise regimen, you will not hit your mark of losing thirty pounds in three weeks. Because of that you will most likely begin to judge your progress based on the false pretense that it is possible to achieve those results. Even if you lose the maximum healthy weight that you could lose in three weeks, let's say ten pounds, you will feel like a failure and possibly give up on your effort, even though you are moving forward and doing extremely well.

This is a vital lesson in all areas of goal setting and skill development. It has a significant impact on your ability to stay fully engaged in the process of achieving any goal you set. It is a powerful asset in any endeavor, whether it is something with easily defined elements, such as learning a golf swing, or something with more abstract and perhaps even constantly changing elements, such as being a good investor or a successful entrepreneur. Don't just pick goals whimsically. Take the time to research and understand them thoroughly so that your expectations are realistic. It is time well spent and will go a long way toward preventing you from sabotaging your own effort. Through your awareness training, try to stay connected to the observer so that you are not just working toward your goals but are staying aware of how you are experiencing the process.

In every moment of your life, you are achieving something, even when it feels insignificant. Understanding the difference between *achieving* versus *achievement* can be very helpful in staying fully engaged in the process and not being tempted to mentally wander into the future. *Achieving* is a verb — and a process. *Achievement* is a noun, a stagnant moment in time. When we reach our goal, we may have a feeling of satisfaction, accomplishment, and maybe even euphoric relief. Goals that require little or no effort don't offer us these experiences because we have nothing of ourselves invested in the process of achieving them. And after we reach a goal, don't we always start to look to the next one? Why is that? It is because we long for that feeling of personal expansion, that feeling of growth and challenge that makes the brief moment of achievement so satisfying. Setting goals using realistic data helps us stay fully engaged in the process of achieving them because we are much less likely to be pulled out of the present by feelings of failure and impatience. More of our energy goes into reaching those goals, and so we work more efficiently. We are not so concerned about time because the experience feels more enjoyable. It's a win-win. Doesn't it make more sense to immerse ourselves in the process of achieving, in which the sense of enjoyment is constant?

Deciding what you will do
in a difficult situation before you are in it
can completely change your experience
of the event when it occurs.

CHAPTER 4

Premeditated Procedures

Escape the Drama

As I mentioned in chapter 2, premeditated procedures are a powerful and dependable way of changing your experience of a stressful situation.

Most of us know exactly what sets us off in a difficult confrontation. Without the correct tools at hand, we can very quickly become absorbed in the emotion of the situation. Instead of being the observer of our thoughts, we become tightly integrated with them, acting out whatever we are feeling. In this state we have relinquished our power as a conscious choice maker. Some people never progress past this state. I would go so far as to say that they're not even aware that a much more refined and powerful state exists. Some people are on the other end of the spectrum, where nothing seems to take control away from them in terms of how they react and how they experience any situation, regardless of how difficult the situation may be. Most of us fall somewhere in between those two extremes.

But as your self-awareness increases through your meditative practice, and as your connection to the observer within you grows, you will start to notice how you respond to confrontational situations *as* they are happening rather than in review. You won't have to try to make this happen; it will be a natural outgrowth of your practice. As I've stated, you cannot change anything without awareness. Awareness must come first. But we all know that simply being aware of something we'd like to change in ourselves doesn't make the change magically happen. It only gives us the opportunity to change, the privilege of choice. To move to the next step and to execute, we need a plan. We need a step-by-step plan customized to our personality to help us deflect the emotional content of a confrontational situation, a comforting place we can retreat to internally, where we can have a moment to take a virtual breath and exercise our power of choice.

In *The Practicing Mind* I talked about using procedures as a way of accomplishing this. Procedures eliminate the need to make decisions, which can be very challenging when you are in a difficult situation. They thin out the emotional energy that can flow so freely in stressful situations, allowing us to stay more fully engaged in the moment. I'd like to share a story about an experience I had many years ago in my business as a concert piano technician that really clarified the value of creating a premeditated procedure for handling a difficult situation.

A very well-known concert pianist was coming into town and was scheduled for a solo appearance that evening at the concert hall. There would be nothing onstage but the performer and the concert grand piano. There would be no orchestra and no other musicians to hide any imperfections in his performance. Life as a touring concert pianist is difficult because unlike most of the other instrumentalists in the orchestra, pianists cannot tour with their personal instrument. There have been some famous artists, such as Vladimir Horowitz, who have toured with their own instrument at times, but in general this is not the case. A violinist brings her violin. A flutist brings his flute. A harpist brings his harp, large as it is. This means that they are performing on the same instrument they have created a bond with on a daily basis as they practice. It is a very personal relationship. Each instrument has its own unique qualities, just like people. It has its own sound and feel, and each instrument will react differently to the same passage being played on it. Needless to say, musicians become very attached to their instruments. They do not take choosing an instrument to play or purchase lightly. For example, guitar players will sit in a room at a music store that may have fifty different guitars hanging on the wall. They will play them one by one, looking for that specific feel and sound that speaks to them personally. It's also common for musicians to spend money to have modifications done to their own instrument to bring out certain qualities that they desire.

Concert grand pianos present a real problem in this

regard. They cost $100,000 or more, weigh close to a thousand pounds, and require a specialized crew and vehicle to transport them. It is simply not practical for a piano soloist to take his instrument with him, so he has to take whatever the concert hall has to offer. Believe it or not, the biggest challenge faced by the piano soloist is not so much the performance itself but finding a piano that is up to the task of responding to his needs. Years ago I was watching the *The Tonight Show*, and the host had invited a famous singer onto the show. The host asked the guest, "As someone who has performed regularly all over the world, what has been your biggest complaint"? The performer responded that he didn't even have to think about it. His biggest complaint was finding a piano that worked and was in tune. It is a universal problem.

A number of sidebars to this particular concert event complicated things for me. For one, I had met this performer several years earlier during a time when he had apparently been suffering from a drinking problem, which made him quite susceptible to big mood swings. I had experienced one of those mood swings firsthand, and I knew what he was capable of. During that episode I had been caught off guard, and fortunately another person was there to witness and validate the performer's irrational behavior and inappropriate insults.

Another issue was the fact that at that particular time the concert hall had not staged an event requiring the concert grand for well over a month. That meant that the piano had sat underneath the stage in an area that was barely climate controlled. Later they rectified this problematic situation, but during that time period the piano could become atrociously out of tune, and the touch weight from key to key could become very inconsistent. A piano is constructed primarily of wood and felt, both of which react to changes in temperature and humidity. When a piano is exposed to high humidity, the wood in the soundboard swells and it moves upward. This stretches the more than 225 strings on the instrument, and they go out of tune. The same high humidity causes the felt hammers to take on moisture. This can make the notes lack clarity and even sound dull. Because each of the eighty-eight hammers on the instrument does not react exactly the same to the environmental changes, you can hear drastic differences from one note to the next as a scale is played. Also, because there are hundreds of hinges in a grand piano keyboard, all of which use felt in their construction, changes in humidity either up or down can cause one piano key to feel more difficult to press down than the adjacent key. For a concert pianist pushing the instrument to its limit in a performance, this can be a serious issue. The plan to eliminate this potential scenario was to put the instrument up on stage the day before so that it could acclimate to the climate-controlled theater; I would arrive at the concert hall the morning of the concert and spend about six hours preparing the instrument for the evening concert. The artist was to come in at five in the afternoon to warm up and to meet with me about any discrepancies he felt were present.

That was not the way it went down.

The pianist had arrived in town the night before. He got up early and was bored in his hotel room, so he decided to go over to the theater and play the piano. Not knowing the potential problems of allowing the pianist to do this, a stagehand let him in and showed him to the instrument. That's when the fireworks started. I received a phone call at about nine o'clock from the stagehand, reciting the colorful articulations the artist had made to describe how big of an incompetent idiot I was and what a piece of garbage the piano was. The stagehand pleaded with me to come in early so that he could escape any further verbal beatings from the pianist, who was clearly boiling with anger.

My first reaction was the one you would probably expect. I was annoyed that the pianist had been allowed to sit at the piano in the first place. Of course the piano sounded terrible and was probably completely unusable, given the situation. Because of the stagehand's poor decision, I now had an incredible hole to climb out of. But that reaction lasted for a fleeting microsecond. Just as quickly I connected to the observer, and my annoyance and anxiety dropped away. I said to the stagehand, "Just try to relax, and tell him I'm on my way."

I took a deep breath and stared at the wall in my office for a moment, contemplating the joyful morning and afternoon I had ahead of me. I could see myself sitting at the piano trying to work with this guy screaming insults at me while I was trying to concentrate. It occurred to me in that moment that I needed a plan, a premeditated procedure that would keep me connected to the observer and allow me to flow through the situation more effortlessly, and not feel like I was on the edge of losing control of my emotions and my professionalism. I needed a plan not to deal with him, since I had no control over his reaction to me, but to make my sense of inner peace untouchable in the midst of his almost certain slamming of me. I asked myself this question: "If I could react any way I wanted in this situation, what would that way be?" I knew that at that moment I had the advantage of not *being* in the situation. I have talked about this with coaching clients and in interviews many times. If you don't know how you would like to react in a situation before you're in it, it's a pretty good bet that you won't be able to figure it out once you're there.

The first thing I did was to visualize the behavior I expected from the performer when we first confronted each other. In my mind I watched him behave as inappropriately as I knew he was capable of. I then decided what my reactions would be, and I practiced responding mentally a few times. I visualized him being abusive and tried to feel what that would be like on the receiving end so that I could rehearse my reactions. I wanted to be familiar with the impulsive responses that I would be tempted to express so that I would see them coming and feel more in control. I gathered my tools and left for the concert hall, and on the way I centered my mind just by paying attention to my breathing and not allowing any anticipatory thoughts to bubble up. You may be saying to yourself, "That sounds really difficult to do!" but when you practice daily thought awareness, you start to identify more strongly with the observer than with your ego. Your willpower grows much stronger. Shutting down thoughts that would not have served my intentions was really not difficult. I walked into the concert hall, went straight to the piano onstage, and began unpacking my tools. At that point the performer was nowhere in sight.

The first thing I wanted to do was to put a rough tuning on the piano. I needed to get it to a point where I could hear what it sounded like so I could start working on the instrument as a whole. A few minutes into that procedure I heard the stage left door open, and I knew the fun was about to begin. Because of where the piano was situated in the wings, I could watch the dark lord marching across the stage toward me, with steam coming out of every orifice of his head. It occurred to me, very briefly, mind you, that this was my last chance to ignite my light saber, but my higher self prevailed and I decided to stay with my original plan. That plan was to put all my focus on staying connected to the observer, to watch the situation unfold as if I were standing on the other side of the stage, and completely separate from his emotional energy.

I reminded myself to expect my own emotional responses to beg to be expressed. I told myself to look at it as just a competitive game. Could I beat the situation with my skill? I also told myself it would be best if I initiated the encounter because I might be able to diffuse his anger to some degree with carefully chosen words. A good plan, though, needs to have contingencies. You anticipate decisions you may have to make ahead of time so that you won't have to ponder your options while reactive emotions are pounding at your door. I told myself that if he jumped the gun and I wasn't able to talk first, I'd let him pay out the line. Like a deep-sea fisherman, I would let him run wild and exhaust his emotional energy while I stood quietly and compassionately looking on. In that way I wouldn't strengthen his energy by feeding it with my own. Fortunately that didn't happen. When he got about eight feet away from me, he just stopped and stared at me.

I stood up, called him by name, and stated that I wanted to profusely apologize to him that someone of his caliber had to tolerate a piano in that condition, even if it was to do nothing more than to run a scale on it. I went on to say that I had been told he would not be there until later that day, at which point I would've had the piano ready for his first look. I continued prattling, mostly because I didn't want him to have a chance to open his mouth and start spitting fire at me. I told him that I was particularly sensitive to his situation, which was the fact that in a number of hours he would be sitting by himself in front of this instrument calling on a lifetime of practice to share with the audience his interpretation of the piece he had chosen to play. If the piano was an inadequate interface for that performance, no one would know that struggle but him. He alone would bear that burden and perhaps even criticism from those unaware of the situation. My job was to have his back and make sure he didn't have to concern himself with that possibility. I told him that I would stay there the whole day and throughout the performance and that we would do whatever we had to do to ensure the piano fulfilled his needs for that evening.

A remarkable and unexpected change in his demeanor began to unfold. I could see the tension leaving his body. His face relaxed, his shoulders dropped, his eyes softened. I knew from years of experience that what he was seeing was that I understood his situation and that I truly cared. I meant what I said. He probably wasn't used to that. I say that because not all piano technicians react like this when they get a difficult artist. Unfortunately, this adversarial scenario is all too normal, and not just in the piano-tuning world. When someone expresses anger toward us, the easiest response is to express anger in return. But emotions are like resonating frequencies. "Like" frequencies strengthen each other, feeding into the overall volume. When one person expresses anger and the other responds with anger, the energy builds. But when one person is visibly calm, the anger has nowhere to go, no way of justifying its existence, and it begins to feel draining and pointless to the angry person.

The first thing this performer did was to softly ask me my name. Then he said, "Thank you, Tom, for understanding my position so well. I am confident in your ability to make the piano what I need. I will be in my dressing room if you need me." That was it. He smiled, turned, and walked offstage. I spent the rest of the day working on the piano, and then I went down to get him. I told him I wanted him to come upstairs and play the piano because we still had some time, and if anything needed to be done I wanted to get right to work on it. He told me that wasn't necessary and that I probably had better things to do on a Saturday evening, he would be fine.

But wait, there's more. Two years later he was back in town at another venue, and I was asked to prepare their piano for him. As I was working, the pianist came out of the wings, saw me, and rushed over to shake my hand. He then proceeded to say, "Tom, it's great to see you again. I am so relieved that you are the technician for this venue. I was concerned that things might not go so well, but now I can relax. I hope you can stick around for the show."

This story demonstrates the power of a premeditated procedure in a difficult situation. When I first got the phone call from the upset stagehand, I had a choice to make. I could've taken the insults relayed by the stagehand personally and driven into the concert hall with something to prove. If I had done that, the consequences would've been far-reaching. The performer's anger would have festered all afternoon and might even have been reflected in his performance that night. The audience would certainly have witnessed a very different performance. I would have been in an agitated state for the rest of the day and probably carried that energy into that Saturday evening and even Sunday. Instead, we both experienced a sense of inner peace, relief, accomplishment, and even a certain sense of joy that always follows the dissipation of anger.

I also gained a valuable technique to put in the bank. The next time a situation like that arose, and I assure you there were "next times," I had a go-to proven strategy that not only took less effort to execute but in some ways was even fun because I was willfully manipulating the situation in a positive way. I also have to believe that this particular performer banked a certain bit of experience himself, and perhaps the next time he came up against a piano that had not yet been prepared, he wouldn't have such a knee-jerk reaction, thus upsetting himself and those around him much less.

So how exactly do we come up with good strategies? The first step is to figure out what types of situations pull you into emotional responses. You can do this both by sitting quietly and reviewing situations that you encounter daily and also by making a note to yourself during the day when you feel a particular situation would be easier to handle if you had a premeditated procedure, a strategy for dealing with it. Some situations will seem obvious, such as having to confront a difficult person, but others may be subtle enough that all you experience is an "I just don't feel like doing this" feeling. As you work at thought awareness training and your connection to the observer grows, you will find that it is easier to identify these situations because you will be more aware of how you are processing the events of your day. I see this routinely with my clients. A few weeks after we start they are amazed at how much they were experiencing during their day internally that they weren't noticing. Once their awareness offers them the privilege of choice, they become anxious to use that power to make their day more enjoyable. As their practice continues they are amazed at how much more energy they have at the end of the day and also at how a situation that used to invoke a fight-or-flight response starts to lose its power over them.

Once you identify the particular situation, acknowledge that it will become the trigger that launches the procedure. The next step is to ask yourself this question: "If I could handle this situation any way I desired, what would that way be?" When you are contemplating the answer to this question, consider what will make you feel the most content and perhaps even impressed with yourself after you execute it. How will you feel twenty-four hours after the situation has passed? The clarity you need to see the optimum actions for you to take is much easier to find when you are outside the situation. That is when you have the time to run several scenarios through your mind, which is exactly what you should do. Weigh the pros and cons for each scenario, and decide which one is best. What you are after here is being able to control yourself in the situation, to stay oriented to the observer, aware of the subtleties of the situation as it unfolds. If you do this, you will be successful.

In my story, the only real control I had over the person I was dealing with was the energy that I put out, and that was enough to control the situation and take it in the right direction. Having a planned procedure made it easy for me to stay fully engaged in the moment-by-moment unfolding of the situation, instead of being the puppet of an emotional response that would not have served me. Creating the procedure beforehand allowed me to practice experiencing the situation before I was in it. This strengthened my confidence in my ability to deal with the situation when it was happening and also had a very strong calming effect. It is always much easier to execute something when you have practiced. In difficult situations such as this, making decisions beforehand about how to handle the situation puts you out in front of the situation itself when it occurs. If you walk into a dark room knowing that when you take your fifth step someone's going to grab your shoulders and say boo, it will have no effect on you, because your knowledge removes the fight-or-flight response. You remain in control of your responses instead of becoming overwhelmed by them.

You may be thinking, "Well, in your situation all went well." But what if it hadn't? As I said above, we also need contingency plans. In my situation, I had considered several possible reactions the performer could have confronted me with. If he does this, I will do that. If he does that, then I will do this. Bringing "what if's" into your premeditated procedure is part of a sound plan. You possess unimaginable personal power and clarity of thought when you can be fully conscious and present in the moment. When you create procedures such as this, even though you may not be able to predict the other person's behavior, you feel confident and prepared for a variety of scenarios. This doesn't mean that no anxious thoughts will arise. At least for a while those thoughts are a habitual response to certain situations, responses you have practiced your whole life. But what you will notice is that the more you connect to the observer within, the more you will merely notice those anxious thoughts instead of becoming completely absorbed in them.

Try to look at situations that normally stress you as an opportunity to play the game. Whether it is a tricky conversation you have to have with someone, a job interview, or someone that you find difficult to work with for whatever reason, creating a premeditated procedure is a very powerful tool. The more you practice it, the less you will have to. What I mean is that in the process of creating procedures you become more connected with the real you, the *you* whom you feel you want to be and can be. You begin to live your life more consciously, more fully engaged, as opposed to ping-ponging through your day emotionally reacting to whatever situations you experience. With practice, it will get easier. You will become so centered in who you really are that you will no longer have to plan your responses, because they will come naturally to you.

Where are you now?
Constantly anticipating a future moment
deprives you of what is unfolding
for you in this moment.

CHAPTER 5

And Then What?

A Mantra for Inner Peace

Preplanned responses are not just useful in difficult situations involving other people. They can also be very effective at helping you reset your perspective when you find yourself craving a future event or circumstance. We spend 90 percent of our time at war with the *process* of achieving our goals. There is simply no peace in this perspective. In the introduction I stated that a global awakening is occurring. Part of this awakening is realizing the futility of our obsession with the moment that we reach any goal. Being fully engaged means fully participating both physically and consciously in what you are doing *right now*. You can't do that if mentally you are always anticipating the experience of a future moment, such as when you acquire the next thing on your wish list or when you cross the finish line of whatever project you are working on. This doesn't mean that you don't allow the moment you achieve your goal to inspire your effort, but if this practice is misused it only serves to create a sense of struggle and a sense of longing that drains you of energy that could be used in serving your progress.

I'd like to share a very useful tool for bringing your mind back to the present moment when it is trying to cling to something that hasn't happened yet. It realigns your perspective of whatever is pulling you into the future and reengages you with the now. When you notice that you are not enjoying this moment because you are craving the moment when you reach your goal, ask yourself, "And then what?" The moment you have what you've been striving for, will everything be perfect in your life? Will you feel fulfilled for a long time, or will the cycle start over again, as it has thousands of times in your life? Will you hunger for a new goal, something new to accomplish, and find yourself back in the same inner state? Asking yourself "And then what?" is an effective reminder that you are missing the pleasure of accomplishing your goal because you are not present in what you are doing. It's a trigger of sorts that dissolves the feeling of "I just need to get to this next place, and then I will feel satisfied."

Human beings have built into their DNA the desire to expand. The human spirit constantly wants to grow, to learn, to refine itself. This is truly one of our best attributes. However, we can all too easily misinterpret this pull as a feeling of being incomplete, and when we do, a sense of struggle arises. This is where the title of this chapter comes into play. If you pay attention to your internal dialogue during the day and examine what you are experiencing in a moment of anxiousness or a feeling of being incomplete, of longing, you will most likely notice that you are trying internally to get to someplace other than where you are in this moment. You are trying to be someplace you have not yet arrived, to experience something that has not yet happened, or to gain something that you do not yet have, such as a material possession.

This kind of misinterpretation is not so easy to cast aside, since we are bombarded by an enormous amount of marketing that serves to nurture this feeling of incompleteness. If you pay attention to your feelings, you will notice this longing idling in the background. There is almost always this sense that something needs to change in our life in order for everything to be just right. No matter what we accomplish or acquire, this feeling has a way of contaminating what we are experiencing right now. Millions of dollars of research are poured into understanding ways to exploit this false sense within us. I recently watched a documentary program describing the psychology that went into the design of a major international airport in Germany. The retail section of the airport was placed in the center, like the hub of a wheel. All the different airline carriers' gates exited into this hub. The designers' research had shown that the flights coming into this airport were generally long. This meant that psychologically the passengers had experienced an extended period of time where they felt they had very little control and therefore would feel a need for a sense of control, which they could attain through purchasing something.

The design of the individual stores was equally well researched. The shape of the counters and the length and shape of the aisles were designed based on the findings of marketing research. Part of that research entailed bringing people in and giving them glasses to wear that had small cameras with lasers mounted on them so that their eye movements could be tracked as they walked through the mocked-up retail centers, which essentially mirrored how the finished retail centers would be constructed. This showed the designers exactly how the layouts affected people's attention. If you are aware that this type of manipulation is being used on you, it has little to no impact on you, but most people just participate in the scenario. For example, one of the major stores in the mall near my house had a floor plan that was deliberately designed to get people lost in the store. Of course, people didn't realize this when the store was first built. Every aisle looked like every other aisle. You would say, "Do I want to go this way?" and shortly thereafter you were asking yourself the same question because you had no idea where you were. People couldn't find their way out of the store. This was great for business because it kept people in the store longer than they intended and made them walk through departments they weren't planning to shop in. However, once you recognized this intentional design (and people did over time) it lost its effectiveness. The people who recognized this would pay close attention to visual cues that would allow them to find their way directly to the department they wanted and then back out of the store.

This feeling of being incomplete may serve business, but it does not serve us. Daily thought awareness training will connect you to the observer more and more, allowing you to be more fully engaged in this moment and to notice this feeling more quickly when it begins. This detached perspective gives you the opportunity to choose your response to those thoughts and feelings instead of just being absorbed in them and carried along by them as an involuntary participant. In that moment when you notice you are experiencing this misinterpretation, say to yourself, "Okay, let's pretend I have this thing, I have gotten to this place, I have achieved this. And then what?"

You will find that the "And then what?" mantra can reset your perspective. It allows you to ask yourself, "Will this feeling that I'm experiencing really go away when I have this, or will I have a short-term sense of gratification that will dissolve back into a feeling of being incomplete the moment I see something else that makes me feel the same way?" You will be able to review how many times you have experienced this cycle and recall what the outcomes were. In that moment, because you are fully present, you will have a deep knowing that this perspective is inaccurate and that whenever you acquire or achieve what you are after, you will long for further expansion. And that is how it should be. Our natural desire to expand who we are and what we are capable of is an asset, not an indicator of what we are lacking. When we experience these feelings we should exhale and say to ourselves, "It's good to know that all my systems are functioning correctly. I can relax and get on with the process of expansion and just enjoy the experience."

I'm not saying that when you truly need something, such as a new car, you shouldn't be fully engaged in the process of acquiring it and enjoy it to the fullest. Nor am I implying that it's wrong to want (and subsequently buy) something that we don't particularly need but that we can afford. You may not *need* a vacation to a specific location, but it's to a place you've always wanted to visit. You may not *need* a new job, but you're ready for a new challenge. What we're trying to accomplish is to be the *observer* of what we are experiencing in this moment, to be fully conscious of how it is making us feel, and to know where that feeling is coming from. In this way we are a conscious choice maker and can choose whether or not to participate. When you have this perspective you know that you are in the present moment and not being manipulated. When you notice yourself feeling incomplete, you have in a sense woken up to the fact that you are not in the present moment and can now bring yourself back to where you have full power.

With practice the feeling of incompleteness becomes the trigger that automatically fires off this simple question: "And then what?" We want this to be our natural response to those feelings. When we first start this practice, we will need to work at it, because we will be swept along by the feeling of need, which can be very strong indeed. Processing this moment as feeling "I can't be happy right now; I just need for these things to happen" is a behavioral habit we have repeated tens of thousands of times. From the wealthiest individuals to the poorest, most of us live in scarcity consciousness as a normal means of functioning. That's why most of our commerce is built around marketing advertisements designed to exploit this mind-set.

If you watch advertisements, you will notice that they start at the goal, meaning that no one is in the process of achieving the goal. I notice, whenever I open up a sailing magazine, that it's common to see people in their midthirties aboard their personal sailboat, which costs three-quarters of a million dollars, with a look that says, "I'm so happy I have this to relieve my boredom." I've seen car commercials that show young parents in front of their expensive home showing off their $45,000 luxury car to their grade-school children as if Santa had dropped it off on Christmas Eve. These types of advertisements are designed to make us feel that we're missing out on something, that all the fun in life is passing us by, that we are lacking and need to step up our game to catch up. We are confronted with it constantly throughout our waking hours.

A young woman named Laura Dekker sailed solo around the world as a teenager. It was her dream to make this twenty-seven-thousand-mile journey alone. Her experience was made into a movie called *Maiden Voyage*. Because I have had a strong interest in sailing, for years I found myself drawn to her story and spent some time researching her. In an interview, she made some comments that bear repeating here. She wasn't interested so much in being the youngest female to circumnavigate the globe in a sailboat by herself. Nor was she interested in breaking some record. She was more interested in the self-discovery she would have through the long hours of solitude, and she also wanted to experience different cultures and interact with people. As I listened to her telling the story of her journey, I was most struck by her comment that one of the things she observed that made the biggest impression on her was the difference in priorities of people as soon as she got away from the "civilized" world (my word). She met families on islands that had almost nothing by our standards, and yet they offered everything they had to her joyously and were happy all the time. She asked them what they would do if someone gave them a million dollars. They responded that they really didn't know because there was nothing they wanted. She couldn't help but notice how the culture that she came from was always obsessed with getting a bigger house, a different car, and more money, and she realized that there was a totally different way of living that by her observation was clearly much more satisfying.

Her story reminded me of a similar situation that I had once experienced. Near my house is a very upscale coffee shop that serves breakfast. One Saturday morning I stopped in to get a quick cup of coffee. As I sat near the front window, I noticed a very expensive sport-utility vehicle pull up and a well-dressed family of four step out. The children were grade-school age. After entering the coffee shop the family sat at the table next to me. The mother took orders for the children's breakfast and went up to the counter. The father stayed at the table. The children were clearly in a good mood and began playfully teasing each other. The father quickly became annoyed with them in a very disproportionate way and reprimanded them, telling them to sit still and just be quiet. Watching this I couldn't help but be struck by the disconnect. Here was someone who had everything he was supposed to have to be happy, and I'm sure he had worked very hard to get it. He was driving a high-status automobile and had a beautiful wife and two lovely children who were so happy that they were all together on a Saturday morning that they couldn't contain themselves. He was wearing a perfectly pressed designer shirt and pants. Yet with all this he was clearly miserable and couldn't enjoy the moment. To be fair, of course I don't know what might have been going on in his life, but I was struck by how he had accomplished everything that we're told will make us happy and yet it was still beyond his grasp to enjoy a simple hour with his family on a Saturday morning.

Remember, our experience of lack is a behavior that we have firmly installed into our personalities, through repetition. We have learned it well, and unlearning it requires first awareness of when we are feeling it and then the desire to repeatedly engage in a different behavior, with the conscious intention of changing how we experience these feelings.

As you work on this empowering change, remember that the practicing mind does not judge your effort in cultivating a new response. It sees only *awareness* and *repetition* with the *intention* toward a specific goal. As long as we are executing that, we are successful. In every repetition we become more powerful in our ability to control how we are experiencing any moment.

One reason for this is that the feelings that create this experience are always rooted in either the past or the future. The simple phrase "And then what?" immediately pulls us into the present moment because we cannot have the awareness to ask ourselves this question if we are experiencing this moment outside the present. When we are in the present moment we have the clarity to remind ourselves that we have experienced this internal longing many times before, that it is an internal feeling that constantly cycles. It is never satisfied for any length of time, no matter what we achieve or acquire. Asking ourselves "And then what?" reminds us of this truth and of the real purpose that it serves. This feeling is there to show us how infinite we truly are and to help us enjoy the experience of becoming.

Change is growth,
and growth is forward motion.
Learn to embrace it in all its disguises.

CHAPTER 6

The "Perfect" Life

Embracing the Experience of Constant Change

Accepting your infinite nature and welcoming the experience of becoming, of constantly expanding, means being open to change. As they say, "The only constant in life is change," and if we want to be fully engaged in any moment, we need to embrace this simple statement. It's not always easy to embrace change. There are times in our lives when we feel sad that change is happening. We want to resist it, even if unbeknown to us it is bringing future happiness into our life. This is a very important point when learning to embrace change in your life that feels difficult, uncomfortable, and even undesirable. Realize that the full impact of what you are going through and how it will enrich your life may not be apparent in this moment. Understanding this can drastically influence your interpretation of what is happening and open you to discovering the full spectrum of what the situation has to offer you.

At my high school graduation a friend of mine told me, as the tears streamed down her cheeks, "It's all going to change now, and I don't want it to. I've loved the time I've had in high school." She wasn't the only one who felt that way. Looking around the football stadium at fellow classmates, some of whom I had known since first grade, I saw expressions displaying everything from giddiness and joy to sadness and nervousness. Many were feeling all those emotions at once, myself included. As I stood there talking, I knew that an era in my life had ended. A few feet away stood another friend of mine. I still had images of him, sitting at the lunch table in first grade with his engineer overalls on, and a freckled face smudged with peanut butter and jelly as he talked with his mouth full of sandwich wide open. It was hard to believe that was just twelve years earlier. Great changes were in store for him; he would become a very successful dentist. As for my teary-eyed friend, I kept in touch with her long enough to witness her life move down a very magical path. She hadn't had that first-true-love experience in high school. Little did she know, as she stood in front of me, that what was speeding toward her was an incredible relationship, a beautiful family, and a job she was passionate about.

It's easy to embrace the idea that experiencing change makes for a perfect life when the change is for the better, when it feels positive and comfortable. But what about when it's not? When change feels difficult, when it hurts, how can we possibly embrace it as being part of a perfect life? When my mother went from being a healthy, vibrant woman to an emaciated cancer victim filled with ever-increasing pain, how could that in any way be construed as positive? This is something I've thought about deeply in order to write this chapter. Even though I know that embracing constant change is part of the perfect life, I also know that reconciling the idea with real life can be challenging. Watching someone I loved suffer and knowing she was leaving me a little more each day certainly didn't instill a sense of perfection in me at the time — anger and frustration, perhaps, but to see anything even remotely positive in that situation would have required a perspective I had not yet developed.

Indeed, at the time of her death I lacked the vision to see the incredibly powerful lessons of love that were unfolding. At that point in my life I was overworked and exhausted from raising a young family. Because my mother never complained about her situation or the pain she was in, if I didn't constantly remind myself of her circumstance, the reality of it all tended to fade into the background as I struggled just to meet my daily obligations. My mother never expressed any fear of moving through the final weeks and days of her life and leaving our physical presence. In fact, when I sat on her hospital bed right after she had been told that her cancer had returned, she looked at me and said, "Did you hear the news?" When I responded yes, she said, "Bummer, but it's okay," and she smiled as if to comfort me.

As time went on my mother remained fully engaged in a process that was inescapable. She was present. When you would sit and talk with her, she made full eye contact no matter how uncomfortable she was physically. She was always an amazing listener. If there is a way to leave this place with poise and dignity, she showed everyone how. Virtually everyone made that comment. So even in the midst of the change that was eroding her body every day, she was expanding everyone else's appreciation of what real courage is and the power of her love for those around her under the most difficult of circumstances. It was more important to her that those around her not suffer because of her situation, and she constantly worked at accomplishing that. My mother, a quiet person by nature, had a way of working her magic simply by being who she was. She didn't need to say much. People felt nurtured simply by being around her. At the time I didn't realize how much she had influenced the way I process life. It wasn't until several years had passed and I would find myself reminiscing about my life with her and how she handled her experience of leaving this life that I began to fully comprehend how much I had gained from this most difficult change in my life.

In the context of her situation there are two kinds of change. I'm speaking about how one's life comes to an end. The change can be abrupt such as in a fatal car accident. There isn't much time in that situation for either the one who is leaving to teach or for those who are left behind to learn. It can be as brief as receiving a phone call, and the loved one is gone. In a lingering illness, however, there is time for the patient to contemplate their situation and for those around them to do the same. This is where my mother's lessons of courage, poise, and strength became so clear in my mind and also helped me realize what I had gained from what otherwise could have been seen as just another tragic loss.

Everything I have just described, the incredible attributes of my mother's personality, became so clearly apparent to me. I learned what quiet courage looks like. I mentioned that my mother never expressed any fear, but I don't know that she never felt it. Her personality was so giving that I fully believe that whatever fear she felt she chose to face on her own rather than burden others with it. The way she stayed fully engaged in her conversations profoundly influenced me, especially with my two daughters; I am reminded to be fully present when they are sharing something about their day with me. Thinking of others first was not only natural for my mom; it made her happy, and that taught me the joy of sharing myself and what I have learned with others, another valuable lesson. There's a paradox here. Difficult changes require inner strength, but at the same time they create inner strength as we experience them. Even now, years later, my mother continues to inspire me every time I evoke her memory. I have gained a lifetime of inspiration from what initially felt like a terrible and painful loss. All these virtues — being fully present when someone is talking to me, selflessness, courage, inner strength, the compassion for others who are going through a similar situation — I gained from a life change that I would never have chosen. I have so much more to offer the people around me now because of how she impacted me.

Change equals growth. That is why it is encoded in

our DNA. Think about it. Would you want to be a first-grader your whole life? Would you want to repeat this day over and over again? Would you want to eat the same thing for lunch every day, always be with the same people, do the same task every day, year after year? We need change to feel content, to feel inspired, to learn. In fact, every change we experience involves learning something, no matter how insignificant it may seem at the time. Change forces us to think, to remember, to evaluate, to be introspective. When we don't experience change we become bored. A life without change would be unbearable.

Some kinds of change we seek out, such as a new skill or a new job. Others we do not, such as death, divorce, and so on. To be fully realized individuals we need the kind of growth that is drawn from both types of experiences. We could say that we seek out positive change and that we try our best to deal with the other type, but in fact both types are positive. We learn powerful skills, such as all that I learned from my mother's passing, only by experiencing such a difficult situation. Because of that experience I am now better at helping others who are going through a similar situation. Even though we tend to avoid such situations, they make us powerful if we pay attention and assess what we are going through. No one wants to experience the pain of a failed romance, but going through that experience allows us to communicate more effectively with someone else who is going through the same thing for the first time. It gives us the power to comfort him or her in ways that would not be possible if we had not had such an experience ourselves. As I have become more fully engaged in my own life I can honestly say that I feel phrases like *difficult situations* or *negative experiences* stem from internal judgments. Those judgments are based on what is comfortable and what is uncomfortable. When we are confronted by change, we need to stay oriented to our *observer*. Otherwise, we label the change based on our emotions, and we quickly become absorbed in those feelings. This robs us of the opportunity to see what the change has to offer us. I will say it again: when you keep up with a meditation practice, your increased awareness of your thoughts will make being observer oriented a much more natural state for you.

I find that when I am fully engaged in the moment and not in the future, which has not yet happened, or in the past, which I have no control over, the opportunity to separate myself from the feeling of "this is comfortable" or "this is uncomfortable" presents itself. In that separateness I can explore my interpretation of whatever change is occurring and why I am labeling it as this or that. I have found that the farther down the road I get in my evolution, the more it all just feels like learning. The first time I was given the opportunity to speak in a large theater about my work, I was very uncomfortable. I jumped at the chance, of course, but it was a big change for me. After I wrote *The Practicing Mind* I did several small talks, but now I found myself on unfamiliar ground. I remember sitting in my dressing room feeling anxious about my ability to remain engaging for the whole talk. When I was called to stand in the wings and get ready, I could tell by the crowd noise that the theater was full. Never having stood onstage by myself in front of so many people, I found a change coming at me big time, and it was creating a lot of fear-based internal dialogue.

Fortunately I was able to very quickly realize what I was participating in. I had always enjoyed sharing my experiences with other people. This was no different, but I was *making* it different simply by interpreting a bigger room with more people as an experience with unknown results. I give this example because even though I greatly desired the opportunity, in that moment I was labeling it as uncomfortable and therefore negative. Realizing this, I was able to reinterpret it as an opportunity to stretch myself and to get to the next level of communicating my ideas. When I saw it from that perspective, I realized that everyone in the audience had paid to hear what I had to say. I was growing and expanding in my ability to speak. That couldn't happen without my giving a talk to a large group for the first time. I relaxed, stepped onto the stage, and thoroughly enjoyed my interactions with all those who were attending both the presentation and the book signing afterward. Going through the transition from being anxious and uncertain to feeling at ease was difficult, but even that is just a label describing my interpretation of the experience. It is still just learning, and as I work at being more fully conscious in each moment, what used to feel like difficult change has softened considerably into a sense of flowing growth.

When we already know how to do something, it feels

effortless. When something is new to us, we are in a state of expansion; we are learning. We are working at the threshold of our abilities, pushing forward into new space. But as we push forward, our threshold also moves forward with us. If we keep this in mind and let go of our expectations, we can fully enjoy this process of expansion. We can stop interpreting the experience of change, of learning, as unpleasant. The trick is to be totally present, to be fully engaged in the process of the change. If we are judging the experience as this or that, we are not fully present because a portion of our consciousness is taken up in the judgment process. When I'm feeling a very strong polarity about a particular change in my life, it's a tip-off that I am not in the present moment, not fully engaged in my experience.

The perfect life *is* constant change because the opposite of change is stagnation, lack of growth. As we saw from the story of my mother's passing, the skills we acquire from what we could easily interpret as difficult changes are some of the most powerful tools we acquire. Like everyone, I face difficult situations regularly. But more and more I find that I am able to welcome circumstances that earlier in my life I would not have wanted to experience because I would have interpreted them as being uncomfortable. I didn't see all that they were offering me — skills I needed to learn, skills that have given me strength in challenging situations and made me more effective at helping others. I now see life's changes not as "easy" or "difficult" but instead as opportunities to expand my ability to function peacefully in all kinds of circumstances.

You cannot master difficult situations without practice. You cannot practice mastery without being in the situation. When you know this, difficulty becomes an opportunity to push past your thresholds.

CHAPTER 7

You Have to Be There

Seeing Opportunity in Moments of Struggle

There is another element of being fully engaged that most of us need to work at being aware of. This behavior, our excessive pull toward the moment when we finally reach our goal, is completely natural. We all experience it. The problem is that it is nurtured to a point of excess by our modern lifestyles and so begins to sabotage our sense of inner peace, our self-confidence, and paradoxically our ability to complete the goals that this behavior is trying to serve. A standard question that I'm asked in interviews is, "Why do we resist being in the present moment? Why do we struggle to focus on the process of what we are trying to accomplish, as opposed to being constantly focused on the moment we crossed the finish line?"

If you think about it, feeling the need to complete things is a survival mechanism that goes who knows how far back in our evolution. I'm sure there were times when we felt if we did not bring down a woolly mammoth in the next twenty-four hours, we were going to starve. Also, feeling the need to reach our goals is part of what fuels motivation. It makes us want to complete our goals instead of setting goals and then falling into a state of apathy about when we reach them. But what we experience today I feel is different. It comes from a toxic level of things that need to be accomplished in a day. It's truly ironic that we have all these modern conveniences that are supposed to make our lives less stressful and easier and give us more free time, yet most of us frequently feel overloaded. This is where the conflict is born. We have a tremendous yearning for closure of any kind. We want that report finished. We want the trip to the grocery store completed. We want the kids picked up from the sporting event. Indeed, we want this day to be over.

Yet being fully engaged in your life, cultivating a practicing mind as a natural way of processing your life, has a beginning, but it does not have an end. It is something we work at all the time, from this day forth. Most of us are uncomfortable with embarking on an endeavor that we cannot finish, that we cannot master, in the traditional sense. Indeed, the idea of engaging in something that is infinite in nature feels overwhelming and even depressing. Interpreting the process with a feeling of "this is going to be on my plate for the rest of my life" reminds me of the feeling I had when I hit forty years old and realized I could no longer eat whatever I wanted and that from then on I was going to have to watch my diet.

But this feeling, this interpretation, is very similar to the trick drawing of a woman that most of us have seen. When you first look at the drawing you see the image of an old hag, complete with warts. But as you continue to stare at it, a subtle shift occurs, and the image of a beautiful young woman appears. It's all in how you interpret the lines on the page. Once you've seen the beautiful woman you can easily see her again every time you look at the picture. The reason being fully engaged is a life's work is because it is boundless in its offerings. Remember, true perfection has no limits. We are never as good at being fully engaged in our life and executing a practicing mind as we could be, and that is a blessing, not a punishment meant to discourage us.

What we struggle with is the sense of making mistakes. Even the word *mistake* conjures up a feeling of failure. We don't want to make mistakes. Mistakes are bad, mistakes are wrong. In my opinion the word *mistake* has really gotten a bad rap. What we call a mistake is nothing more than a teaching tool. In fact, from my perspective mistakes, in the traditional understanding of the word, don't exist. They are just points of learning flowing past us. When viewed in this way they can be seen as clues to helping us find the treasure we are seeking. When viewed in the traditional manner, they feel more like obstacles to reaching our goals. Very subtle shifts of perspective can be very powerful. I do want to make clear that here I am talking about our efforts in personal growth, not mistakes that have dire consequences such as leaving a loaded handgun on the kitchen table with a three-year-old running around the house unsupervised.

I have told a story many times about an event that affected me at least as much as it affected the person I was working with. A young golfer once asked me to help her overcome some mental struggles she was having when things started to go poorly during a tournament. This young woman had proved her athleticism numerous times and was one of the best golfers in the state, but when her physical game began to let her down, her mind became her enemy instead of her ally. Normally, in the event she was competing in, caddies were not allowed, so she had to carry her own clubs. She was alone on the golf course with no one but herself to help resolve any physical or internal conflicts that arose.

When I started meeting with her, our main goal was to help her play well in a qualifying tournament that was a year away. If she did well in that tournament she would move up to the next level, with a chance to go on and possibly play in a professional event as an amateur. We met numerous times throughout the year and discussed strategies for how to handle the natural pull toward negativity that she felt came over her when she wasn't playing well. When the qualifying tournament finally arrived, she found that she was allowed to have a caddy and asked me if I would do that for her, thinking that having me there would give her an edge. When I first pulled up to the range and saw her hitting balls, I could already see the nervousness in her swing. It was as if instead of relaxing and allowing her talent to shine forth, she was trying not to make a bad swing.

Her first drive went right, missing the fairway. This was very uncharacteristic of her, and it set up an eroding lack of confidence. Initially I didn't want to talk much because I was concerned about increasing the internal dialogue that I knew was already going on in her head. This was difficult for me because I could sense her emotions as we walked down the fairways. She felt she had prepared for this tournament very well, and here she was, completely off her game, brokenhearted and seemingly unable to right the ship. On or about the sixth hole she had no chance of winning. Ironically, I was beginning to think that my presence was making the situation worse because I felt as if, on top of everything else, she was trying to not vent her emotions because she didn't want me to see her behaving that way. I knew I had to do something.

As we were walking down the fairway, tracking down her errant shot, I asked her why she had asked me to work with her. Her response was simple. "I asked you to work with me so I could figure out what to do in a situation like this when nothing is going right." Her response gave me an opening, and so I posed this question to her: "How do you think you do that?" Staring straight ahead, she responded, "Tom, I honestly have no idea. I have tried everything I know, and nothing is working." After waiting a moment I said, "I think you're missing the intent of my question. You asked me to help you learn how to deal with yourself on the course when everything is going wrong.

We can talk about all kinds of strategies to help you deal with that situation, but in order to execute them you have to be in the situation. If you want to learn how to play in the rain, it has to be raining. If you want to learn how to play in gusty conditions, the wind has to be gusting, and if you want to learn how to deal with *yourself* when the wheels have come completely off, you have to be in that situation, and guess what, you're there. This is what you have been training for. So let go of winning the tournament or even placing. This tournament isn't going to determine whether you get a college scholarship or if you go on to become a professional golfer. But it is giving you an opportunity to prove to yourself that you can turn it around. Focus on that, and show me what you've got."

She had been seeing the situation one-dimensionally. When she stopped looking at the situation from the perspective of what it was taking away from her and started looking at the opportunities it had to offer, everything changed. It was as if somebody had flipped a switch. It involved the same player, the same golf swing, the same golf course on the same day, but her subtle shift in perspective turned it into a game that she was going to win, and win she did. Within a few holes she was striping the ball the way she knew she could, and she walked off the course feeling as if she acquired a skill that would serve her the rest of her career.

This story demonstrates the reason I called this chapter "You Have to Be There." As you work with all that we have discussed in this book, understand that there are no mistakes, in the traditional sense of the word. There is just a continual refining of your actions, with clues along the way. If you say to yourself, "I want to be fully engaged in my life in every moment. Then I know I will be happy," you have missed the point and are setting yourself up to constantly feel like a failure. As you work at refining the practicing mind and being fully engaged in your life, you will constantly improve but you will not be able to do it all the time. It is an infinite challenge, and to think otherwise would be to set a goal with incorrect data. If, however, you can self-correct, if you can just notice when you are not being fully engaged, without any sense of judgment, without saying, for example, "I should be better at this by this point in time," and bring yourself back into this moment, then you are completely successful, just in that act.

In a way it's ironic. When you start out on this path, you have the lowest skill level, the highest expectations, and the harshest self-judgment. As your skill level increases, your awareness of your potential for growth expands exponentially, and your judgment of your progress continually lessens. Your mind quiets down, and you are content with where you are on the path right now. Your patience with yourself, your life, and those around you grows without your trying to make it happen. Unfortunately, we have been taught that if we don't feel as if we are struggling, we are not getting anywhere — the whole no-pain-no-gain syndrome. Through my continued work at being fully engaged in my life, I have found the opposite to be true. When I'm feeling a sense of struggle, I know something is askew and I'm not fully engaged in the process of what I'm trying to accomplish. And when I look back at things I used to feel were mistakes, I honestly don't feel that way anymore, or at least I have no sense of regret attached to them. They were just clues along the way that have helped me become who I am and get where I am today — and that is a wonderful place. As we all move down this path and become more fully engaged in our lives, we find not only that life has more to offer us but also that we all have more to offer each other. It's a great place to be heading.

About the Author

Thomas M. Sterner is the founder and CEO of the Practicing Mind Institute. As a successful entrepreneur, he is considered an expert in Present Moment Functioning, or PMF™. He is a popular and in-demand speaker who works with high-performance industry groups and individuals, including athletes, helping them operate effectively in high-stress situations so that they can break through to new levels of mastery.

As an expert Present Moment Functioning coach, Sterner has brought clarity to thousands regarding how they can accomplish more with less effort in the least amount of time and with greatly reduced stress. Top media outlets such as NPR, Fox News, and Forbes have sought his advice. He is the author of the bestseller *The Practicing Mind: Developing Focus and Discipline in Your Life* (New World Library, 2012).

Prior to founding the Practicing Mind Institute, he served as the chief concert piano technician for a major performing arts center, preparing instruments for the most demanding performances. During his twenty-five-year tenure as a high-level technician, he personally worked for industry giants such as Van Cliburn, Luciano Pavarotti, André Watts, Ray Charles, Fleetwood Mac, Bonnie Raitt, Tony Bennett, Wynton Marsalis, and many more. An accomplished musician and composer, he has also worked in the visual arts and as a recording studio engineer.

In his downtime Tom is a private pilot, avid sailor, and proficient golfer. He lives in Wilmington, Delaware, and enjoys spending time with his two daughters and in his recording studio.